Contents

Introduction   **v**

Classroom Environment and Community of Learners (Teacher Rubric)   **xx**

Classroom Environment and Community of Learners (School Rubric)   **xxii**

CHAPTER 1   **Creating Beautiful and Inviting Classrooms**   **1**

Fostering Print-Rich Classrooms and Hallways   **7**

Organizing Work Spaces, Desks, and Materials   **12**

Creating and Displaying Anchor Charts   **24**

Evaluating Your Classroom Environment   **28**

CHAPTER 2   **Forming a Community**   **32**

Establishing a Culturally Responsive Classroom   **32**

Modifying the Classroom Environment for
English Language Learners   **38**

Differentiating Learning for All Students   **43**

Creating a Community of Learners   **52**

CHAPTER 3   **Getting to the Essence of Learning and Teaching**   **61**

Creating Student-Centered Classrooms   **62**

Promoting Student Talk   **64**

Demonstrating, Guiding, and Conferring   **66**

Facilitating Student Learning   **69**

Teaching Effectively Through Classroom Management   **73**

CHAPTER 4   **Fostering Independence**   **83**

Creating Opportunities for Choice   **84**

Providing Scaffolding   **86**

Building Stamina   **87**

CHAPTER **Becoming a Reflective Practitioner**

5

Looking Inward 93

Looking Outward 95

Appendix: Professional Books I Want to Read 123

Acknowledgments 125

References 129

Enriching Classroom Environments

RUBRICS AND RESOURCES FOR SELF-EVALUATION AND GOAL SETTING

FOR **LITERACY COACHES, PRINCIPALS,** AND **TEACHER STUDY GROUPS, K–6**

Bonnie Campbell Hill *&* Carrie Ekey

HEINEMANN
Portsmouth, NH

Heinemann
361 Hanover Street
Portsmouth, NH 03801–3912
www.heinemann.com

Offices and agents throughout the world

The authors and publisher wish to thank those who have generously given permission to reprint borrowed material:

"We Have All Come from Somewhere" from *A Sea of Faces: The Importance of Knowing Your Students* by Donald H. Graves. Copyright © 2006 by Donald H. Graves. Published by Heinemann. Reprinted by permission of the publisher.

"Model of Learning" from *The Whole Story* by Brian Cambourne. Copyright © 1998 by Brian Cambourne. Published by Scholastic Inc. Reprinted by permission of the publisher.

Library of Congress Cataloging-in-Publication Data
Hill, Bonnie Campbell.
    The next-step guide to enriching classroom environments : rubrics and resources for self-evaluation and goal setting for literacy coaches, principals, and teacher study groups, K–6 / Bonnie Campbell Hill and Carrie Ekey.
        p. cm.
    Includes bibliographical references.
    ISBN-13: 978-0-325-01058-8
    ISBN-10: 0-325-01058-7
    1. Language arts (Elementary). 2. Classroom environment. 3. Reflective teaching. 4. Educational evaluation.   I. Ekey, Carrie. II. Title.
    LB1576.H3516 2010
    372.6—dc22   2009046481

Editor: Kate Montgomery
Production: Lynne Costa
Cover design: Jenny Jensen Greenleaf
Cover photograph: Antonella Sassu, American School in London
Interior design and typesetter: Gina Poirier
Manufacturing: Steve Bernier

Printed in the United States of America on acid-free paper
14 13 12 11 10 ML 1 2 3 4 5

Introduction

Carrie and I have the best jobs ever. We visit fabulous classrooms, learn alongside teachers, pick up new ideas, and then share them with other teachers in schools around the world. In this book, we share some of what we've learned about creating enticing classrooms in which teachers and students are enthusiastic participants in a learning community. Our goal is to help teachers and schools reach further and higher in their effort to improve learning for all students and make school a joyful place to learn and teach.

We zoom in specifically on ways in which the physical, social, and emotional environment can best support literacy. Join us as we pop into some exemplary elementary school classrooms and talk about some of the ideas we've learned (some of which you probably use in your own classroom) and the inspiring books we've read (some of which you've probably read as well). Classroom vignettes, photographs, book lists, annotations, quotes, and questions along the way will help you assess *what works* well in your classroom and decide *what's next* for your own professional growth.

Who We Are

Bonnie

After teaching in elementary schools in Boulder, Colorado, and Seattle, Washington, I returned to graduate school, got my doctorate in education, and began to teach at the university level. Instead of guiding thirty students each year, I could guide thirty teachers, each of whom had twenty to thirty students. The teachers I worked with in the Seattle area shared what they were doing, and I was often able visit their classrooms, learning alongside them. I began presenting at state and national conferences, often in conjunction with these outstanding classroom teachers. Eventually, I began writing professional books in order to share what I was learning and the amazing work these teachers were doing. Many of the teachers I met through my college classes contributed ideas and even coauthored some of these professional books.

With the publication of my books came invitations to speak at conferences for international schools in various parts of the world, followed by invitations to work at some of these schools. Since I spent third, fourth, and fifth grade at an international school in Istanbul, Turkey, and have a deeply ingrained love of travel, I jumped at these incredible opportunities. At this point I've worked with over fifty international schools and spoken at conferences in Central and South America, Eastern and Western Europe, Africa, Asia, and the Middle East. I hope to share with you some of what I've learned about successful classroom environments from teachers and students in classrooms around the world.

Much of my initial work in schools involves "putting the pieces together"— linking a school's philosophy, standards, curriculum, instruction, assessment, and reporting. That's a lot to tackle at once, so after discussions about what pieces of the puzzle each school has in place, the administrators, teachers, and I usually create a four-year plan for implementing change, new ideas, and best practices in literacy. Since my time with each school is usually limited to a few days or a week, my friend and colleague Carrie Ekey provides follow-up support to these schools based on their specific needs as they expand their expertise in literacy instruction and assessment.

Carrie

I officially retired from the Denver metro area's Jefferson County School District in 2002. I've been an elementary classroom teacher, a lead district staff developer, and a curriculum specialist. I was also a core coordinator and instructor in a master's program for teachers at Regis University in Denver. Since Bonnie first convinced me to begin consulting in international schools overseas, I've visited over twenty-five international schools. After Bonnie's initial visit to schools, I help the staff reach a common understanding of a balanced literacy program, as well as help develop literacy curriculum. Often I help administrators develop a vision, goals, and a long-range plan. I then introduce literacy instructional strategies to teachers through workshops and demonstration lessons and develop common understanding and practices around literacy instruction and assessment in grade-level team meetings. I sometimes work on improving classroom libraries and often hold literacy workshops for parents.

In addition to my ongoing work with international schools, I was a consultant-in-residence for one year at the International School of Beijing and for two years at the Hong Kong International School. I've worked harder in the last eight years than ever before and hardly feel "retired"!

Most recently I've developed initial units of study in literacy for schools that don't have the staff to do this themselves. I've also begun to train literacy coaches for international schools with the support of NESA (the Near East South Asian group of schools). I recently completed the first iteration of this two-year training program with twenty-five teachers from fourteen international schools in twelve countries. This fall, I began training a second cadre of twenty additional international school teachers who will meet in various countries four times over the next two years. Many of these teacher leaders and coaches have contributed ideas and photographs for this book.

What We Do

In our ongoing tag-team work with schools, we continue to build on each other's work, share ideas, and swap travel tips. Between us, we've racked up a slew of frequent-flyer miles. The twenty- or even thirty-six–hour flights are physically exhausting, and we don't stop running from the minute we hit the ground until we fly out. Since our jobs are fairly unusual and the examples we will share come from teachers and classrooms around the world, we'd like to begin with a short explanation of our roles and the context for our work.

Most of our careers have been spent working in classrooms in the United States, and we continue our connections with many of these teachers, especially those close to our homes in Denver and Seattle. These teachers have contributed many of the examples and photographs in this book. However, a great deal of our time recently has been spent working with international schools. These K–12 schools are most often created for the expatriate communities living in these countries, and most have an American curriculum and classrooms much like ones down the street from our houses. These international schools are essentially a miniature school district with a director (superintendent) and a high school, a middle school, and an elementary school. The teachers are primarily from the United States, Canada, Great Britain, Australia, and New Zealand, although some are from other countries as well. The schools in Africa and South and Central America have a higher percentage of teachers from the local country.

The students in these schools come from all over the world. Some are members of embassy families, some work for non-governmental organizations (NGOs), and some have parents who work for huge international companies. Postings are usually for two to five years, although some families stay longer. The number of local students varies greatly from school to school, although it's usually less than 20 percent. We have also had the privilege of occasionally working with local schools, such as two amazing bilingual (Arabic/English) schools in Bahrain and Saudi Arabia. Each school has its own challenges related to student and staff turnover (sometimes as high as 50 percent!), access to resources, the added responsibility of teaching the local language to students, access to professional learning experiences like conferences, and politics.

However, the most astonishing aspect of our work is that the major educational challenges are the same, whether it's a classroom in North Dakota, Paris, or Tanzania. Good teachers around the world all want to know how to improve their teaching to better meet their students' needs. The dedicated teachers we work with in Denver, Colorado, and in Doha, Qatar, all want to keep up with current research and best practices.

This book was a daunting undertaking. Carrie and I were often emailing each other from around the globe as I worked with a school in Paris and she was busy doing classroom demonstrations in Indonesia. Thank heavens for email and SKYPE phone calls! In the three years it took us to write this book, we've been interrupted by a tornado and blizzard (Colorado); a typhoon (Hong Kong); an earthquake (Indonesia); the death of Carrie's mother; and innumerable power outages, computer glitches, and flight disasters. Despite the challenges of weather, technology, and daily life, we persevered because of our deep desire to help teachers and our belief in the value of this project. Our floors, dining room tables, and nightstands have overflowed with stacks of professional books. We enlisted the help of two knowledgeable colleagues, Sandy Garcia Figueroa (a principal in Arizona) and Laura Benson (a literacy consultant in Colorado), to help us read and annotate hundreds of professional books and DVDs. We've tried to create a "metabook" in which we synthesize everything we've ever read about classroom environments and list the most helpful resources about each topic. We've also gone into classrooms and emailed the wonderful teachers we know in order to gather stories and photographs showing what these cutting-edge ideas look like in practice. Our stack of permission forms for the hundreds of photographs we collected is three feet high! So although our names are on the cover of this book, it's truly been a worldwide collaborative project and journey.

As we wrote, we discovered that it was simply too confusing for readers if we wrote in two voices, so Carrie graciously allowed me (Bonnie) to write in the first person. I've occasionally woven in Carrie's stories in her own words, but much of the text is a combination of our experiences and knowledge.

About This Book

Carrie and I originally began this literacy-focused project intending to include writing, reading, assessment, and reporting. However, as we worked with teachers and schools, we realized that the conditions for learning were vital to the success of any literacy initiative. We learned the hard way that our presentations on reading or writing workshop rarely took root in schools in which teachers had not read about the latest developments in the profession or considered why and how to teach responsively. Literacy initiatives sometimes fell short when the majority of students were pulled out of the classroom for English language support during instructional time. And sometimes the swirl of politics and personalities within a school created an atmosphere of resistance and animosity toward any ideas we presented. It became clear that a healthy, respectful classroom and school environment was fundamental to change and a necessary foundation before we could help schools build meaningful and long-lasting literacy initiatives. Rather than tackling learning in all content areas, we decided to narrow the scope of this book to how the classroom environment and literacy learning interact.

About the Staff Development Rubrics

To support teachers and schools, Carrie and I developed a rubric describing an exemplary classroom environment that provides materials, structures, and instruction in a way that fosters independence and creates a community of learners. When we first introduced the rubric, some teachers were very accurate—if anything, underestimating their abilities. Others who were clearly novices marked themselves as "leaders." Obviously, the rubric couldn't stand alone. Some teachers "didn't know what they didn't know." We wanted to flesh out the rubric with classroom stories, professional books and DVDs, and photographs.

Thus began our three-year journey as we tried to articulate and capture exemplary practices. We've created additional rubrics for writing, reading, assessment and evaluation, and portfolios and reporting. We hope to explore those topics in forthcoming books. This first book focuses on the classroom environment, since it's the foundation on which good teaching and assessment is built.

Shekou Administrators Treena Casey and Bob Dunseth Fill Out the School Version of the Rubric

If you are a literacy coach, assistant principal, or principal, you will read this book through a different lens. Therefore, we've also created a version of this rubric specifically for literacy coaches and principals. As you try to help teachers in your building expand and deepen their knowledge of best practices, you may want to use the "school" version of the Classroom Environment and Community of Learners rubric to ascertain *what works* for your staff and *what's next* so that you can provide time, resources, and professional development opportunities based on those goals.

The Teacher Rubrics in Action

I met Kathy Sandler when she was teaching at the Shekou International School in China, and I had just created the first staff development rubrics. She now teaches fourth grade at the Taipei American School in Taiwan, and recently used the updated version of the Classroom Environment and Community of Learners rubric (see pp. xx–xxi) to evaluate her own teaching and set professional goals:

> When I first used this rubric, I had been teaching for ten years and knew that staying current with best practices was important not only for my teaching career but also for my students' learning experiences while in my classroom. I was somewhere between an apprentice and practitioner in the learning and teaching and independence categories on the Classroom Environment and Community of Learners rubric. I mostly led the discussions in my classroom from the front of the room, and literature groups usually studied novels that I had selected and for which I generated discussion questions.
>
> While attending Reading and Writing Institutes at Columbia University's Teachers College, I learned that reading and writing steps could be broken into "moves" the students could understand and follow. I became a fan of Janet Angelillo's books *A Fresh Approach to Teaching Punctuation* (2002) and *Making Revision Matter* (2005). These books really influenced my teaching and helped me improve my anchor charts with explicit teaching points for revising using mentor texts. I also read *A Writer's Notebook: Unlocking the Writer Within You* (1996) and *Craft Lessons* (2007), by Ralph Fletcher and JoAnn Portalupi, and learned how to teach the qualities of writing more intentionally. My school began using the reading and writing continuums created by Bonnie Campbell Hill (2001), which provide clear goals for instruction and differentiation.
>
> To improve my classroom management skills, I turned to *The Daily 5* (2006), by Gail Boushey and Joan Moser, and *Knee to Knee, Eye to Eye* (2003), by Ardith Davis Cole. These books influenced the way I teach

behaviors in my class through modeling and instilling student ownership. Using the Lucy Calkins *Units of Study for Teaching Writing* (2006), I learned the importance of the architecture of my minilessons. Providing clear teaching points and active engagement have helped improve my writers' workshop and better prepare my students for independent work after my minilessons. I now see myself as somewhere between a practitioner and leader on the classroom environment rubric. This past year I held book clubs throughout the year and provided opportunities for my students to select books based on interests and lead their own discussions. After reading *Practical Punctuation*, by Dan Feigelson (2008), I tried his inquiry model for teaching punctuation and plan to continue using it this year.

At my current school, there are many teachers at a grade level, which requires teamwork. Collaboration among my colleagues improves the curriculum we offer our students. It enables us to be more efficient and effective, as well as learn from one another. I am now a leader in the reflective practice category of the Classroom Environment and Community of Learners rubric; I enjoy sharing my experiences and knowledge with my teammates and supporting the sharing that takes place within our team and our school.

As we move forward in this digital age, the way we teach and even what we teach will continue to change. In one of her units of study for writing, Lucy Calkins says, "When you think you are done, you've only just begun." I think this applies to my learning as a teacher. This rubric is a valuable tool for reflection and allows me to celebrate how I've grown and to set goals for my next steps as a learner and teacher.

As you can see, using the rubric helped Kathy establish goals for moving from teacher-directed to student-centered instruction. She chose one content area, writing, and focused on how to set up a classroom environment that supported student-centered learning. Next, she chose the goal of classroom management and again went to professional resources to begin to understand how classroom management could establish and support this type of literacy instruction. Finally, her own professional learning led her to be looked on as an instructional leader in her school. She now sees her professional learning as a lifelong journey that will take her into other new areas, such as technology, in the future.

The curriculum director at Shekou had high praise: "Kathy is passionate about literacy and is a truly reflective teacher. She creates a learning environment that is warm and inviting, and fosters in her students a love for learning. She pursues, shares, and models current research and is an inspiration to her colleagues."

Kathy Sandler Uses a Rubric for Self-Evaluation and Goal Setting

The School Rubrics in Action

Before I work with a school, I ask for a copy of their language arts curriculum documents, their standards, and their report card. This gives me a picture of the literacy *content* the school has developed. Then I ask the principal to take me on a tour of all the elementary classrooms. I look at the amount of print in a classroom, the arrangement of desks and learning spaces, the type of instruction taking place, and the amount of teacher and student talk. When possible, I chat quietly with a few students about what they are learning. Sometimes I find a gap between what's on paper and actual practice; other times I'm thrilled to see a match between what I've read and what I see. These walkthroughs and my conversations with teachers, students, and principals provide a picture of the *context* of literacy learning, which is just as important as the *content*. In addition to examining school documents and walking through classrooms, I use the staff development rubrics to help me ascertain the specific strengths and needs of each school.

One school I worked with had a yearlong reading focus. They had sent me their reading standards and curriculum, but it wasn't until I visited the school that I discovered that students were still ability grouped. These reading groups most often stayed together all year, and little accommodation was made for individual differences. In addition, the amount of reading and the expectations differed significantly between groups. Placement in the groups was based on teacher recommendations and one yearly reading test. Instruction was often text driven rather than in response to student needs. In most classrooms, student desks were arranged in rows and instruction was teacher centered. Classroom libraries were sparse and students had very few choices about the books they read or opportunities for collaboration.

This school was at the apprentice stage in the first four categories of the Classroom Environment and Community of Learners rubric. Since most teachers worked in isolation and only reluctantly participated in professional development, they were at the novice stage in the reflective practice category. Research clearly shows that instruction should be flexible and responsive and that all children should have equal opportunities and access to quality instruction and books. Therefore, during Carrie's follow-up visit, her first steps were to present research about ability grouping and to offer examples of ways to group students flexibly based on their assessed needs. She also gave classroom demonstrations to highlight the power of student talk and intentional minilessons. The school instigated focused grade-level meetings and initiated their first professional book studies.

Over the next two years, Carrie coached the administrator and a team of teacher-leaders as they explored and shared ideas about classroom environment, grouping, inclusion, and gradual-release instruction. She also presented some workshops in which she modeled best practices and launched some small-group collaboration. Within two years this school provided professional development focused on establishing an inviting classroom environment and differentiating reading instruction; hired a core group of teachers who understood best practices in literacy instruction; encouraged a core group of teachers to attend summer literacy institutes conducted by the Teachers College Reading and Writing Project; hired a literacy coach; began organizing a book room for small-group instruction and revitalizing classroom libraries for independent reading; and initiated professional book studies and conversations about writing instruction. They have made great progress on their literacy journey.

I visited another school where teachers had spent a year examining research about the teaching of reading, then developed a common philosophy statement and essential agreements about how reading would be taught at each grade level. Teachers read professional books about the gradual release model of instruction and discussed differentiation, grouping, and how to teach reading through whole-group and small-group instruction and individual conferences. Student desks were clustered in groups and classrooms were student centered, with many opportunities for discussion and collaboration. Classroom libraries contained neatly organized tubs of developmentally appropriate books in various genres about a range of topics. Grouping was flexible and needs based, and students had a voice in their writing and reading topics.

This school was at the leader stage in three rubric areas (classroom, learning and teaching, and independence) and at the practitioner stage in the remaining categories (community and reflective practice). Carrie and the leadership team decided to focus on four areas for the school's next steps: examining research and models relative to modifying instruction to include their English language learners (ELLs); promoting more collaboration and sharing *between* grade levels; initiating and supporting peer observations using protocols; and conducting professional book studies based on the needs of the staff. Carrie also helped the school's literacy coordinator evaluate and expand classroom libraries so that teachers could differentiate their reading instruction. Within two years this school had provided professional development related to differentiating instruction, especially for ELLs; supported cross-grade–level conversations about writing instruction; undertaken a few peer observations; and conducted a number of professional book studies geared to teachers' needs and interests. In this school, there was a match between learning and instruction and the classroom environment.

Warning!

Because Carrie and I created these staff development rubrics as tools for teachers to evaluate their own teaching and set their own goals, we want to emphasize that they should *not* be used for evaluation by the administrator. The rubrics can help principals, coaches, and teachers identify best practices, but as soon as they take on the aura of evaluation, they lose all their potential for change. Teachers won't be honest about their strengths and areas for growth unless they are part of a supportive and risk-taking environment in which everyone is viewed as a learner.

Key Components

Five essential aspects of classroom environment and community form the framework on which to build effective literacy teaching and learning:

- ▶ Classroom environment (physical environment)
- ▶ Community of learners (social and emotional environment)
- ▶ Learning and teaching (instructional environment)
- ▶ Independence (instructional environment)
- ▶ Reflective practice

These components of effective classroom design and instruction form the five rows on the Classroom Environment and Community of Learners rubric (see pp. xx–xxiii), and each is discussed in a chapter of this book.

Chapter 1: Creating Beautiful and Inviting Classrooms

Have you ever visited a classroom that was so organized and appealing you wanted to walk around and take pictures? What about that classroom made it so kid-friendly and appealing? Chapter 1 is about the physical aspects of classroom environment and community. It describes how you can intentionally create a beautiful and inviting classroom that reflects your philosophy and supports learning and independence.

Chapter 2: Forming a Community

How many students do you have in your classroom who are still learning English or who have cultural or learning differences? Do you feel you're able to modify your instruction, classroom environment, and materials in order to support the learning of these students? You may have a three- or even four-year grade-level span of reading and writing abilities in your room. How do you provide instruction for that wide range of learners? Chapter 2 is about the social and emotional environment in your classroom. It includes ideas about how differentiation and inclusion can help you meet the needs of *all* your students, especially those with cultural, linguistic, or learning differences, in order to create a supportive community of learners.

Chapter 3: Getting to the Essence of Learning and Teaching

Would you say that your classroom is more teacher centered, more student centered, or somewhere in between? Chapter 3 explores the role of teacher talk and student talk in classrooms and the role of teachers in demonstrating, guiding, and conferring with students. It concludes with a discussion about classroom management and other ways to facilitate student learning.

Chapter 4: Fostering Independence

Have you visited a classroom where students are so independent that you could chat with the teacher for ten minutes while they kept on working?

With all you're expected to cover each year, how can you still provide students with enough choice so that they are invested in and motivated by learning? Some teachers provide such strong modeling and helpful mini-lessons that their students are able to internalize those strategies and apply them independently in new contexts. Chapter 4 explores ways in which teachers can provide choice within a teaching framework, as well as ways to help students develop stamina and independence. Chapter 3 and Chapter 4 address the instructional aspects of the classroom environment and community.

Chapter 5: Becoming a Reflective Practitioner

We hope that you see yourself as a reflective practitioner. The final chapter discusses ways to reach out to colleagues in order to grow professionally by collaborating, observing peers, reading about the teaching profession, writing, mentoring colleagues, and participating in professional development. The chapter concludes with some final considerations about being a reflective practitioner.

Book Lists, Annotations, Photographs, and Professional Book Log

Each chapter includes lists of professional books linked to every descriptor in the Leader column of the Classroom Environment and Community of Learners rubric. I provide annotations for all of these books on my website (bonniecampbellhill.com) and will add new resources as they are published. Carrie and I want to thank her husband, Glenn, who helped take and organize hundreds of photographs of classrooms from around the world that are also included on my website (click on the link to this book and you will be prompted with an access code). We also want to thank my techie sons, Bruce and Keith, who designed the database so we could share these photographs and annotations with readers. We're incredibly fortunate to have such in-house (literally!) expertise. This has truly been a labor of love for us, for teachers around the world, and for our families!

If, like me, you read with pen in hand, you may want to place a checkmark next to the professional books you've already read and asterisk (*) by the books you want to read next. You can then list the professional books you want to read on the form in the Appendix. Some of you will fill up the whole page in no time! If you want to learn more about some of the books, you can read the annotations on my website to determine which books will be most helpful.

If you are like me, you probably anguish over which professional books to purchase with a limited budget. I want to know as much as I can about a book in order to ascertain if it will address a particular need I have for my learning and next steps. I want to know the grade range, the topics covered in the book, and if this book would be helpful. Most publishing companies now provide book annotations on their websites, however, most of these annotations still do not have enough information for me to make my final decision about whether or not to buy a book. Carrie and I often *booktalk* the best professional books we read and are often asked by teachers, coaches, and principals for advice about helpful books on specific topics. For this reason, Carrie and I— with help from Sandy Figueroa and Laura Benson—have written over a hundred annotations that we feel will help you decide which professional books and DVDs to add to your personal library about classroom environments. We have included annotations and bibliographic information on my website (www.bonniecampbellhill.com) as a free resource to educators who have bought this book. I encourage you to look up the annotation for *Spaces and Places* by Debbie Diller to try it out. It will only take you a few minutes and I believe it will hook you into using the database. I promise I will add new resources as they are published, which will help you to keep up to date with all the latest professional books even after you read this book.

I also know that a picture is worth a thousand words. When Carrie and I present, teachers often ask for copies of the photographs of classrooms that we include in our PowerPoint presentations. They tell us that actually *seeing* real classrooms and literacy practices makes the ideas more tangible and inspiring. For these reasons, we have posted additional photographs of stunning classrooms and literacy instruction on my website. I believe that just looking at them will inspire you as you rethink your own classroom and discover ways to support your community of learners. I would encourage you to go to my website, click on the link to this book, then explore the photographs of beautiful classrooms and hallways. Aren't those images inspiring? We hope that in addition to this book, my website and database will provide additional inspiration and ongoing support for your professional learning.

What Works? What Next?

As you read this book, you may want to examine the appropriate rubric to determine your (or your school's) areas of strength (*what works?*) and the concepts you might want to explore further (*what's next?*). The corresponding row of both the teacher and the school versions of the rubric are included at the end of each chapter. We hope that the interspersed "ponder boxes" with self-evaluation questions make it easy for you to pause and reflect on your or your school's teaching and learning.

Highlight the specific descriptors in the rubric that reflect your practices and knowledge, pat yourself on the back, and celebrate all that you already have in place. Then, use a different-color highlighter to indicate areas for improvement. Or you might want to use one color this year for aspects you already have incorporated and use a different color next year as you implement new ideas and dig deeper into a topic as a way to visually track your professional growth. After making those changes, observe your students and evaluate the effect the changes have had on their learning.

Some of you may decide to read one or two books on your own during the school year or during your vacation. If you have colleagues with similar interests, you may want to read a book with another teacher, in grade-level teams, or maybe study a professional book with a cross-grade–level group of colleagues. If you're a real techie, you may want to keep a blog about the books you read. If you are a principal or literacy coach, you might choose a few books to read, as well as facilitate grade-level or small-group professional book studies about how to create an exciting classroom environment and foster a community of learners.

One final warning. As you read about all these fabulous books and ideas, it's very easy to become overwhelmed. Remember that no one teacher implements all these ideas and no one could possibly read all these books. Whenever you start feeling inadequate, take a deep breath and remember that change takes time. It's important to start small. The only way to continue the literacy journey is to take one step at a time. All the ideas and books we share are exciting, but pick just one or two intriguing ideas to try and one or two books to read. Once those are under your belt, you can come back and pick a new goal. Remember that your ultimate purpose is to create a beautiful and inviting classroom that will motivate students to learn more joyfully and effectively.

And one final tip. Learning is so much more fun when you work alongside a friend. Work with a colleague or your literacy coach (if you're lucky enough to have one). Celebrate when you try something new; when new ideas work, share your learning with other colleagues. If you are a principal or coach, celebrate when teachers take risks and incorporate new ideas, and encourage and structure opportunities for collaboration and sharing.

Photographs on Front Cover and Chapter Openers

Front cover: Antonella Sassu, American School in London, England

Chapter 1: Melissa White and Karen Snyder, American Embassy School, Delhi, India

Chapter 2: Jemma Hooykaas, Singapore American School

Chapter 3: Megan Sloan, Cathcart Elementary, Snohomish, Washington

Chapter 4: Megan Sloan, Cathcart Elementary, Snohomish, Washington

Chapter 5: Pam Pottle, Roosevelt School, Bellingham, Washington

Classroom Environment and Community of Learners (Teacher Rubric)

Teacher and Grade Level: **Date:**

Check the boxes that apply, perhaps using a highlighter to mark some or all of the specific descriptors. Use the back for comments.

NOVICE	APPRENTICE	PRACTITIONER	LEADER
Classroom			
☐ Desks are arranged in rows; I have created or purchased most of the material on the walls/bulletin boards; the student work displayed is mostly homogeneous	☐ There are a few areas for group work; I have created or purchased some material for the walls/bulletin boards, some student-created work is displayed	☐ Tables or desks are arranged for small-group work; there is a comfortable area for whole-class meetings; walls/bulletin boards are filled with varied examples of student work and class-generated charts summarizing minilessons	☐ Comfortable, inviting areas have been specifically designed for whole-group, small-group, and individual work; tables or desks are arranged for small-group work; walls/bulletin boards are filled with displays of student work, environmental print, and class-generated charts that change over time and reflect student reading and writing, inquiry, and the learning process; students consistently refer to the charts as they work
Community			
☐ There is little modification of classroom work for needs of different learners; my program for ELLs and learners with special needs is primarily "pull-out" and/or limited; students tend to work in isolation or in a competitive way	☐ There are minimal modifications for ELLs and learners with special needs (e.g., I tell them to read books two or more times); my program for ELLs and learners with special needs is primarily "pull-out" but includes some "push-in" and inclusion; I have some rapport with my students; there is a general sense of community; I introduce some cooperative learning activities	☐ Some of my instruction is differentiated and modified for ELLs and learners with special needs based on systemic school-wide practices (e.g., I use visual cues when reading aloud); my program for ELLs and other learners with special needs is a combination of inclusion, "push-in," and "pull-out"; ESL/ELL and resource teachers sometimes work in my classroom; students support and encourage one another and sometimes collaborate; I focus on building a sense of community	☐ My teaching and materials are culturally responsive and inclusive; I differentiate and modify my instruction for ELLs and learners with special needs; ELLs and learners with special needs have mostly an inclusion and "push-in" program, but there is a "pull-out" program as needed for some students; my back-and-forth communication with the ESL/ELL teachers and resource staff is clear and cooperative; I encourage a risk-taking and collaborative environment in which students support and encourage one another in a respectful, thoughtful, literate community of learners

Learning and Teaching

NOVICE	APPRENTICE	PRACTITIONER	LEADER
☐ My classroom is teacher centered; my teacher talk predominates; the classroom is mostly silent or noisy with unproductive talk; I am usually at the front of the classroom or behind my desk; my classroom management is lacking or focused solely on discipline; students raise their hands and I call on them to respond; students primarily respond to short-answer questions	☐ My classroom is mostly teacher centered; my teacher talk predominates but I also lead some student discussions; the classroom is often quiet or sometimes noisy with unproductive talk; I sometimes meet with small groups; I am sometimes at the front of the classroom or behind my desk; my classroom management focuses mostly on discipline; I guide discussions and students raise their hands; questions and problems are usually directed to me	☐ My classroom is mostly student centered; the classroom is beginning to buzz with appropriate student conversations; I ask questions that facilitate learning; I use some intentional gradual-release techniques; I sometimes demonstrate, guide, or confer; my classroom management is mostly effective and focuses on student independence; I provide some opportunities for discussions, collaboration, and problem solving; students are beginning to direct their conversation to peers as well as to me; students mostly respect and support one another	☐ My classroom is student centered; student talk is evident throughout the day in large- and small-group interactions, as well as during individual conferences; I intentionally use language and questions to facilitate learning; I teach responsively using gradual-release techniques; I usually demonstrate, guide, or confer; my classroom management is highly effective and focuses on student independence; I am a facilitator; I provide many opportunities for high-level discussions, open-ended questions, problem solving, partner and small-group work; students are respectful and supportive of others

Independence

NOVICE	APPRENTICE	PRACTITIONER	LEADER
☐ I select topics for reading and writing; student work is mostly worksheets and workbooks; student engagement is minimal	☐ I occasionally offer students some choices of writing topics and some choices of books for independent reading; I assign many whole-class projects; students are sometimes actively involved in learning	☐ I offer some student choices for reading, writing, and inquiry; I am beginning to provide scaffolding based on students' needs; students are actively involved in learning; students work independently for short periods	☐ I provide many opportunities for choice to support engagement; I provide many opportunities for student self-selected reading, writing, and inquiry; I provide scaffolding based on students' needs; students' extended engagement leads to stamina and independence

Reflective Practice

NOVICE	APPRENTICE	PRACTITIONER	LEADER
☐ I work mostly in isolation and rarely collaborate with my colleagues; I participate reluctantly in required professional development activities and workshops	☐ I share ideas informally and collaborate with a few colleagues; I participate in required professional learning opportunities and book studies	☐ I share ideas and collaborate with my colleagues; I am part of a cohesive grade-level team; I exchange informal peer observations with a few trusted colleagues; I read material about best practices; I sometimes participate in optional professional development and book studies; I often share new ideas with peers and sometimes implement new ideas	☐ My school faculty is a collegial team; there is strong collaboration between grade levels; I exchange formal and informal peer observations with several colleagues; I actively participate in professional development and ongoing book studies; I collaborate, mentor other teachers, and take on leadership roles; I continually implement new ideas and seek to improve instruction; I am a reflective practitioner

Classroom Environment and Community of Learners (School Rubric)

Teacher and Grade Level: **Date:**

Check the boxes that apply, perhaps using a highlighter to mark some or all of the specific descriptors. Use the back for comments.

NOVICE	APPRENTICE	PRACTITIONER	LEADER
		Classrooms and Hallways	
☐ In most classrooms, desks are arranged in rows; bulletin boards, walls and hallways contain mostly teacher-created or purchased materials; some homogeneous student work is displayed	☐ In most classrooms, there are a few areas for group work; bulletin boards, walls and hallways contain some teacher-created or purchased materials; some student-created work is displayed	☐ In most classrooms, tables or desks are arranged for small-group work; in most classrooms, there are comfortable areas for whole-class meetings; in most classrooms, walls/bulletin boards are filled with varied examples of student work and class-generated charts summarizing mini-lessons	☐ In all classrooms, comfortable, inviting areas have been designed for whole-group, small-group, and individual work; in all classrooms, tables or desks are arranged for small-group work; walls/bulletin boards and hallways are filled with displays of student work, environmental print, and class-generated charts that change over time and reflect student reading and writing, inquiry, and the learning process; in all classrooms, students often refer to the charts as they work
		Community	
☐ In most classrooms, there is little modification of classroom work for needs of different learners; programs for ELLs and learners with special needs are primarily "pull-out" and/or limited; in most classrooms students tend to work in isolation or in a competitive way	☐ Teachers make a few modifications for ELLs and learners with special needs (e.g., students are told to read books two or more times); programs for ELLs and learners with special needs are primarily "pull-out"; in a few classrooms, there is some "push-in" and inclusion; most teachers have some rapport with their students; in most classrooms, there is a general sense of community; most teachers introduce some cooperative learning activities	☐ In most classrooms, teachers differentiate and modify some instruction for ELLs and learners with special needs based on systemic schoolwide practices (e.g., teachers use visual cues when reading aloud); in most classrooms, programs for ELLs and learners with special needs are a combination of inclusion, "push-in," and "pull-out"; ESL/ELL and resource teachers work in most classrooms; in most classrooms, students support and encourage one another and sometimes collaborate; most teachers focus on building a sense of community	☐ In all classrooms, learning and materials are culturally responsive and inclusive; teachers in all classrooms differentiate and modify their instruction for ELLs and learners with special needs; ELLs and learners with special needs have mostly inclusion and "push-in" programs, but there are some "pull-out" programs as needed for some students; back-and-forth communication with the ESL/ELL teachers and resource staff is clear and cooperative; teachers in all classrooms encourage a risk-taking and collaborative environment in which students support and encourage one another in respectful, thoughtful, literate communities of learners

NOVICE	APPRENTICE	PRACTITIONER	LEADER
Learning and Teaching			
☐ The majority of the classrooms are teacher centered; in most classrooms, teacher talk predominates; classrooms are mostly silent or noisy with unproductive talk; teachers are usually at the front of the classroom or behind their desks; in some classrooms, classroom management is lacking or focused solely on discipline; in most classrooms students raise their hands and teachers call on them to respond; in most classrooms students respond to short-answer questions	☐ Learning is mostly teacher-centered in most classrooms; in most classrooms, teacher talk predominates but teachers also lead some student discussions; most classrooms are often quiet or are sometimes noisy with unproductive talk; in some classrooms, teachers sometimes meet with small groups; teachers are sometimes at the front of the classroom or behind their desks; classroom management mostly focuses on discipline; in most classrooms, teachers guide discussions and students raise their hands; in most classrooms, questions and problems are usually directed to teachers	☐ Most classrooms are student-centered; most classrooms are beginning to buzz with student conversations; in most classrooms, teachers ask questions to facilitate learning; in most classrooms, teachers use some intentional gradual-release techniques; in most classrooms teachers sometimes demonstrate, guide, or confer; in most classrooms, classroom management is mostly effective and focuses on student independence; in most classrooms, teachers provide some opportunities for discussions, collaboration, open-ended questions, and problem solving; in most classrooms, students are beginning to direct their conversation to peers as well as to the teacher; in most classrooms, students mostly respect and support one another	☐ Learning is student-centered in all classrooms; in all classrooms student talk is evident throughout the day in large- and small-group interactions, as well as during individual conferences; all teachers intentionally use language and questions to facilitate learning; in all classrooms, teachers teach responsively using gradual-release techniques; teachers in all classrooms usually demonstrate, guide, or confer; in all classrooms, classroom management is highly effective and focuses on student independence; in all classrooms, teachers are facilitators; teachers in all classrooms provide many opportunities for high-level discussions, open-ended questions, problem solving, and partner and small-group work; in all classrooms, students are respectful and supportive of others
Independence			
☐ In most classrooms, teachers select topics for reading and writing; in most classrooms, student work is primarily worksheets and workbooks; in most classrooms, student engagement is minimal	☐ In most classrooms, teachers offer students some choices of writing topics and some choices of books for independent reading; in most classrooms, teachers assign many whole-class projects; in most classrooms, students are sometimes actively engaged in learning	☐ In most classrooms, teachers offer student choices for reading, writing, and inquiry; in most classrooms, teachers are beginning to provide scaffolding based on students' needs; in most classrooms, students are actively involved in learning; in most classrooms, students work independently for short periods	☐ Teachers in all classrooms provide many opportunities for choice to support engagement; there are many opportunities for student-selected reading, writing, and inquiry throughout the school; in all classrooms, teachers provide scaffolding based on students' needs; in all classrooms, extended engagement leads to stamina and independence
Reflective Practice			
☐ Teachers mostly work in isolation and rarely collaborate with their colleagues; most teachers participate reluctantly in required professional development activities and workshops	☐ Teachers share ideas informally and collaborate with a few colleagues; there is some cohesion with some colleagues or within some grade levels; some teachers participate in required professional learning opportunities and book studies	☐ Many teachers share ideas and collaborate with their colleagues; most grade-level teams are cohesive; there are some informal peer observations among a few trusted colleagues at some grade levels; most teachers read material about best practices; most teachers participate in optional professional learning opportunities and book studies; many teachers share new ideas with peers and begin to implement new ideas	☐ The school faculty is a collegial team; there is strong collaboration between grade levels; there are formal and informal peer observations within each grade level; all teachers actively participate in professional development and ongoing book studies; many teachers collaborate, mentor others, and take leadership roles; all teachers continually implement new ideas and seek to improve instruction; there is a school climate of investigation, exploration, and reflection

Creating Beautiful and Inviting Classrooms

Walking through a school before I begin my work there gives me incredible insight into its culture and the teachers' understanding of literacy practices. It helps me adjust the workshop I present, decide which activities I introduce, and determine which resources I offer. Here are a few of things I hope not to see:

▶ Students' heads bent over worksheets.

▶ Teachers lecturing formally in the front of the room, a teacher's guide in hand.

▶ (Heaven forbid!) Teachers checking email at their desk.

On the other hand, these are things I love to see:

▶ Teachers modeling their own writing on chart paper.

▶ Students working on authentic reading and writing projects.

▶ Students who can tell me what they are learning.

▶ Teachers kneeling alongside small groups of writers.

▶ Teachers reading aloud from a recently published picture book.

▶ Organized tubs of books.

▶ Classroom charts that reflect the minilessons that have taken place.

The former Deputy Chancellor of New York Schools, Carmen Fariña, refers to walkthroughs like this as *glory walks*, a term that connotes celebration rather than evaluation. Therefore, I make sure to validate strong teaching, highlight pockets of excellence, and celebrate some of the solid instructional practices I see.

I hope the classrooms I describe in this chapter are so inviting and literacy rich that they knock your socks off! But they are more than just beautiful; they're also based on research and sound theories about teaching and learning. They aren't like those "coffee-table books" people place strategically in the living room but never read, but more like well-loved paperbacks, filled with sticky notes and frayed covers. They are real classrooms led by real teachers, filled with the hum of student talk. I want you to be able to picture their cozy book areas and bulletin boards showcasing student work. Carrie and I spent three years gathering photographs of classrooms that exemplify the concepts described in this chapter. A few are included in this book, and there are many more on my website (bonniecampbellhill.com). Our goal is to help you "know what you know" and "know what you don't know" about effective classroom environments and how best to create a community of learners. We hope you are inspired!

Creating your classroom environment is a critical piece of your educational plan. It's the framework on which you build your instruction. Therefore, how can you consciously design your classroom to enhance and support learning? How does your room reflect your beliefs about teaching and learning? Marlynn Clayton and Mary Beth Forton, in *Classroom Spaces That Work* (2001), inspire us with this insight: "A classroom that is not centered on educational beliefs is a room of disconnected details, a room of convenience rather than purpose. It is our focus on our educational beliefs that aligns all the details of the room, blending them together seamlessly to create the whole" (8). You know immediately when you step inside a vibrant, literacy-rich classroom, because learning has been made visible and public.

Beliefs About Creating Beautiful and Inviting Classrooms

❶ Our classroom environment and design communicate our philosophy, goals, and values.

❷ Learning is enhanced when the classroom environment is organized, comfortable, and inviting.

❸ Children learn best in a student-centered classroom in which materials, displays, and the room arrangement are intentionally designed to promote both collaboration and independence.

❹ Classroom spaces and materials should be designed to accommodate students with special needs.

❺ An authentic print-rich environment supports students in their growing independence and literacy.

❻ Children feel more ownership in a classroom when they have opportunities to help design and decorate the spaces.

❼ Children learn more in classrooms in which student work is continually displayed and changed in order to reflect and celebrate their effort and growth.

❽ Collaboratively created anchor charts that reflect units of study and inquiry promote active learning.

Figure 1.1

Everything is authentic, organized, and purposeful. How many of the beliefs listed in Figure 1–1 are reflected in your classroom?

When my son was first learning to play soccer, his coach held practices at a school soccer field. The field was familiar to the boys, and at the beginning of each practice they helped set up the equipment, laying out the soccer balls in an organized space, placing their own personal soccer bags in another designated spot, and posting their team flag in a prominent position on the field, claiming space for the duration of the session. The boys took pride in this regular setup, and because it was so organized, no time was lost looking for balls or misplaced equipment. Their time could be spent learning to play soccer. During the very first practice, the coach outlined strategic spots on the soccer field for individual skill drills, small-group plays, and skirmishes. In two sessions, the boys learned their roles and where they needed to be at certain times. It was inspiring to watch them move from space to space independently, rather than waiting for the coach to tell them what to do next.

The coach didn't have walls or other space on which to display the team's efforts, but he did pass out weekly bulletins to all the parents in which he explained the skills and strategies the boys were learning and celebrated some of the specific achievements of the previous game. Therefore, we knew what our child was learning, even if we couldn't attend all the practices or games. Many parents found they could talk about soccer with their sons more easily and understood the game better because of this extra information. Nowadays, coaches of my friends' kids set up websites where they post the skills they're working on, as well as video clips and photos from their games. But even more important than the organization and communication my son's coach provided was the way he modeled strong sportsmanlike conduct for his players and their parents in his interactions before, during, and after each game.

The type of physical environment and structure that works on the soccer field applies equally in our classrooms. Strong teachers set up comfortable environments in which materials are clearly organized. The routines and rituals they set in place create a sense of structure and predictability that promotes independence. They display student work, celebrate growth, communicate with parents, and model effective reading and writing strategies. When effective learning environments are not intentionally designed, student motivation wanes, materials are lost, behavioral issues arise, time is wasted, instruction becomes diluted, and parents become concerned. Nor is it just about making physical changes; it's important to understand *why* these changes are necessary and *how* they better support student engagement, collaboration, and independence.

What impressions do visitors get when they walk into your classroom? As Michael Gladwell points out in *Blink* (2005), a lot of information is processed as part of a first impression and it's often fairly accurate. Do they trip over lunchboxes and coats that cascade onto the floor? Is your desk the first thing they see? Or do they see a low table with cushions, a cozy meeting area, or an inviting couch for reading next to bookshelves filled with neat rows of book tubs? Does the bulletin board have thirty tulips that all look alike, or does student work reflect each child's uniqueness?

Shelley Harwayne, the principal of the Manhattan New School, suggests that a school should be the most beautiful building in a neighborhood. She writes, "Our classrooms look different because we value beautiful and interesting spaces over bland rooms filled with row after row of desks. We have high standards not only for our work, but for our surroundings as well" (1999, 42). Schools and classrooms *should* be welcoming places in which teachers and students enjoy spending time together. Some of the classrooms I've visited are so friendly and comfortable that I want to linger longer. The physical environment is appealing. There are inviting areas where the whole class can meet, cozy book nooks that maybe include a couch or rocking chair. These teachers have worked hard to clear the clutter; they have organized spaces in the classroom for coats and lunchboxes, as well as introduced and practiced management routines to keep them organized. They've also added a few personal touches—pillows, plants, lamps, low tables, and strings of lights—so that their classrooms feel almost like home.

My two favorite books about classrooms are Debbie Diller's *Spaces and Places: Designing Classrooms for Literacy* (2008) and Debbie Miller's *Teaching with Intention* (2008). The "Diller and Miller books" both include color photographs of classrooms, along with suggestions for changing ordinary classrooms into beautiful spaces. Teachers love the "before and after" photos that provide glimpses of cluttered book areas transformed into beautiful new classroom libraries, now organized with neatly labeled book tubs.

When *Spaces and Places* was first published, I made the mistake of sharing my copy of the book, along with my rave reviews, at the start of a workshop. Never again! Pockets of excited whispers rippled from table to table as teachers passed the book around. I now share the book at the *end* of a workshop. The teachers at that first school were so thrilled by the book, which is jam-packed with color photographs, that they begged to keep my copy, even though I had made notes in the margins and highlighted ideas. Now I bring a copy with me whenever I work with schools. Teachers beg to take the copy home after the workshop, promising to pass it along in a day or two. I've never had a book fly out of my hands so quickly. Teachers often come in over the weekend to redo their room. On Monday, they pull me down the hallway to see their transformed classroom as they bubble over with pride and delight. Unlike some professional books that take time to digest, I've found that this book leads to immediate results. Get one copy and place it in your staff room and see what happens!

The first year I taught, I inherited a classroom from a teacher who had been in the same room for twenty-five years. She was a collector, and it took me two years just to clear out the old birds' nests, broken microscopes, and (giving away my age!) stacks and stacks of purple dittos. I could have used Debbie Miller's advice in *Teaching with Intention* about sorting through clutter: make three piles—things to keep, things someone else might want, things to throw away. It can be fun to tackle your messy shelves or rethink a space that doesn't seem to be working well with a colleague, taking turns in both classrooms. Be sure to take pictures; it's gratifying to document the transformation.

Have you ever watched *Trading Spaces* or *Extreme Home Makeover* and wished Paige Davis or Ty Pennington could come into your school and do the same for your classroom? Gail Boushey and Joan Moser, known as "The Sisters," lead a class every fall called Trading Spaces, in which they help a lucky teacher transform his or her classroom. They also have a DVD called *Simply Beautiful* (2006) in which they demonstrate how they work with teachers to rethink the design and appearance of a classroom. It begins with a guided tour of Joan's classroom as they explain their design philosophy, which is based on the most current brain research. If you're a new teacher about to set up your first classroom, if you've recently moved into a new room, or if you're just hoping to spruce up your current room, this DVD will give you some practical and creative ideas for designing an effective learning environment. You can also catch "The Sisters" in action on the Choice Literacy website (choiceliteracy.com) as they work with classroom teachers to enhance their book areas, improve classroom lighting, and display children's artwork effectively.

It's important to remember *why* we would even want to redesign our classrooms. We want our rooms to reflect our philosophy and practices in order to teach effectively and efficiently. In *Spaces and Places* (2008), Debbie Diller reminds us: "Restructuring classroom spaces often leads to improved instruction. It provides the structure necessary for instruction to be more successful and allows kids to add their stamp and make the room theirs" (3). And isn't that our goal?

In addition to an organized and literacy-rich physical environment, I look for classrooms that are student centered and collaborative. I hope to find rooms filled with the buzz of student talk around learning, rooms in which students are actively engaged and teachers are busy modeling, interacting, and conferring. When I talk with teachers, I want to pick up on their joy in teaching and their knowledge of each student as a unique and special individual.

If you want to learn more about creating beautiful and inviting classrooms, check out one or more of the resources listed at the end of this chapter and explore the annotations on my website (bonniecampbellhill.com). If you're a literacy coach or principal, you may want to jigsaw-read these books with a group of teachers, focusing on a different person's room each month, exchanging ideas and working collaboratively to enhance the look and feel of the classrooms in your school.

Ponder Box for Teachers

- What do students and visitors see when they enter your classroom?
- Are there cluttered areas that you might want to redo?
- Is the area for coats and lunchboxes tucked away and organized?
- Could you add lamps, plants, pillows, couches, or low tables to create ambience?

Ponder Box for Coaches and Principals

- How do you support teachers in creating organized and inviting classrooms?

- What kinds of furniture and materials are you providing to help teachers clear their classrooms of clutter?

- Could you add comfortable chairs, couches, and lamps in hallways and nooks to create welcoming areas outside classrooms?

- If you wish to have more consistent classroom environments, what things will you need to keep in mind when purchasing items and planning reconstruction?

Now that I've applied the broad brushstrokes, I'll use smaller brushes to capture three specific aspects of beautiful classrooms:

▶ Print-rich hallways and classrooms

▶ Organized work spaces, desks, and materials (including classroom libraries)

▶ Anchor charts

Fostering Print-Rich Classrooms and Hallways

The student work, charts, and displays that you hang on the walls reflect your beliefs about teaching and learning. A red flag goes up anytime I visit a school after the first week of classes and see bare hallways devoid of student work. I'm also concerned when I enter classrooms in which worksheets are displayed or all the students' writing or artwork looks alike or the bulletin boards are filled with commercially made holiday decorations. In *Classroom Spaces That Work* (2003), Marlynn Clayton and Mary Beth Forton comment wryly that "it's not uncommon to see classrooms where teacher-created or store-bought displays and decorations cover much of the space, making students feel like they've stepped into a party store rather than a classroom" (101).

Children need a print-rich classroom in which the shelves, walls, and cupboards drip with authentic print. Children immersed in posters, anchor charts, labels, and signs see literacy being used for authentic purposes. When we display their work, their peers, parents, teachers, principals, and visitors all become potential audience members. A print-rich environment provides children with authentic printed resources and validates and celebrates their work, fostering both a sense of pride and a feeling that they are part of a reading-writing community.

Bulletin Boards

One of the many radical things I heard Shelley Harwayne say when I visited the Manhattan New School was that they did not allow any products from teacher stores. Just that one change gave their school a totally different feel; the halls were overflowing with work by and for students, and displays were authentic rather than "cute." It's a radical step to do away with commercial bulletin-board material and may not be something your whole school is ready to tackle, but it might be something to consider in your classroom.

Believe it or not, even the way you set up bulletin boards can have a direct impact on teaching and learning. Bulletin boards should be places where you display children's work or charts that you create together as a learning community. Displays of student reading, writing, and thinking (as well as artwork, math, and other content-area work) are a link with recent learning and a reference point for further instruction. They make learning public and affirm and celebrate students' hard work. They also showcase student learning for other teachers, the principal, family members, and other visitors.

When you move into a new house, you have to unpack your boxes before you start hanging pictures. Once you've set up the tables and learning areas in your classroom, how do you decorate the walls and bulletin boards? Do you spend hours creating borders and displays? What if instead you let your students own the walls?

Megan Sloan wants her classroom to look inviting to her new students and their families, so she creates a bulletin board at the beginning of the year labeled *We Love All Kinds of Books* on which she displays a variety of book jackets. She also posts inviting poems that become part of her initial shared reading lessons. Her students know from the get-go that this is a classroom with a teacher who loves to read and share books and that they will learn to do so as well. The first day of school, Megan asks her students to create self-portraits, which immediately fill up another wall. (As more charts and artwork are created, the students' self-portraits are stored in their portfolios.) If students have helped create the bulletin boards, they are more likely to "read the walls" and use the displayed material as part of their learning process.

赵乔瑾

Qiaojin (Joy)
Mary O'Reilly's class,
International School
of Beijing, China,
Grade 3

Sherri Ballew,
Sunnyside Elementary,
Marysville, WA,
Grade 4

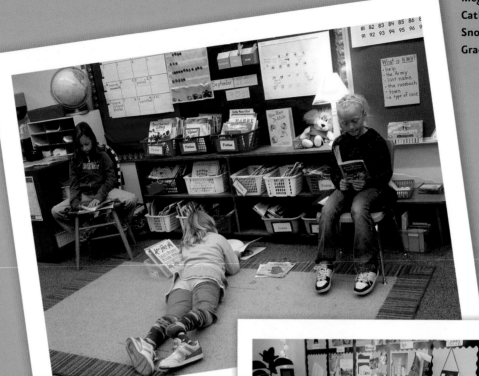

Megan Sloan,
Cathcart Elementary,
Snohomish, WA,
Grade 2 and 3

Trish Tynan,
The American International
School of Mucat, Oman,
Grade 2

Cathy Hsu,
Taipei American School,
Taiwan, Grade 5

Maria Puntereri,
American School
in London, England,
Grade 2

Linda Lee,
Willard Elementary,
Spokane, WA,
Multiage (ages 6, 7 and 8)

Linda Lee,
Willard Elementary,
Spokane, WA,
Multiage (ages 6, 7 and 8)

Mary O'Reilly,
International School
of Beijing, China
Grade 3

Jo Kember,
American School
in London, England,
Grade 1

Chad Johnson,
The American
International School
of Muscat, Oman,
Grade 5

Megan Sloan,
Cathcart Elementary,
Snohomish, WA,
Grade 2 and 3

Eliza Lewis, Hong Kong
International School,
Hong Kong, China,
Grade 1 and Literacy Coordinator

Suzanne Lituchy, American School
in London, England, Grade 3

Anita Gallagher,
Singapore American
School, Singapore
Grade 3

Megan Sloan,
Cathcart Elementary,
Snohomish, WA
Grades 2 and 3

Avid reader in
Debbie Woodfield's
class, Singapore
American School,
Grade 1

Danielle Scully,
American School
in London, England,
Grade 2

In Doriane Marvel's first-grade classroom, there is one bulletin board for literacy and another for the content areas. Student work holds center stage. Each student has a designated space on both bulletin boards. Kids can choose work to display, as long as it includes a reflection about why they chose the piece. As new samples are posted, the earlier work is placed in their portfolios. This keeps students thinking about the goals they set during conferences and helps them monitor their progress.

Environmental Print and Labels

If you've been around preschoolers, you know the power of the "golden arches." Each time they see this piece of environmental print, they proudly yell out, "McDonald's!" They love to eat there, but they also love to show you that they can "read" the sign. Reading signs is an indicator of "print awareness" and signals that youngsters are beginning to show an interest in the world of print that surrounds them. They don't formally learn phonics before they learn to read *Cheerios*, *Toys 'R Us*, *STOP*, *Eject*, or even the signs for the girls' and boys' restrooms. Through constant exposure to authentic print, they learn to recognize these signs. Young children also may have learned a few letters of the alphabet by watching television shows like *Sesame Street* on which the everyday household items and common animals shown alongside each letter soon have children making a connection between the letter and the corresponding initial sound of the object or animal. Many children, older ones included, will value and be more likely to use environmental print in classrooms if they have helped create signs in the block area that shout *DO NOT TUCH* or posters advertising an upcoming *Mother-Daughter Book Club*.

In preschool, kindergarten, and first-grade classrooms, environmental print provides a rich opportunity for literacy learning. For instance, Ranu Bhattacharyya plasters labels on everything in her kindergarten classroom—plants, windows, doors, and the play kitchen sink. She illustrates topic ideas with rebuses for young writers who are just beginning to read. She provides materials for signs in the block area, menu pads in the play area, and a pad of sticky notes near the play phone in the drama area. She also displays digital photographs of her students at work on various projects so that visitors see the process as well as the beautiful work her kindergartners create.

Linda Lee and Mary Hammond team teach a primary multiage classroom with a high percentage of English languages learners (ELLs). They encourage parents to spend time in their classroom and are inundated with visitors. They also believe it helps learners to know the rationale behind each activity. For all these reasons, they often label the art, literacy, and inquiry projects that fill up every inch of their classroom. For instance, when they are doing a folktale unit focused on story elements, a sign above the students' story maps contains an explanation for students, parents, and visitors. Next to hallway displays, signs reveal that students are studying the text features of nonfiction as they write research reports about animals. Students see and hear the language of literacy, but parents and visitors also know that Linda and Mary have a clear vision and purpose for the activities in their busy primary classroom.

As an alternative to the ubiquitous store-bought alphabet strips, invite your students to write the letters and illustrate the alphabet themselves. If you're an upper elementary teacher, students can display their printing and cursive handwriting skills, as well as their artistic talents as they decorate their alphabet card with an appropriate item. In an early childhood classroom, students could use digital cameras to take pictures of objects for each letter or make alphabet charts of words in the languages represented in the class. Upper-grade students can also make signs announcing upcoming events or performances.

Ponder Box for Teachers

- How much time do you spend before school starts working on your bulletin boards?

- What displays could you create at the beginning of the year that would reflect your beliefs about literacy and engage your students?

- How could you involve your students in creating some of the bulletin boards, word walls, and alphabet charts?

- Where can you display student writing? responses to literature? content-area work?

- Do all student pieces look alike or does each student's uniqueness shine through?

- Do you have a bookshelf for books and poems the class has written?

- If you teach a primary grade, do you have print materials in all areas (blocks, play kitchen, dress-up area, drama center, etc.)?

- Do you have labels around the room?

- How do you display the alphabet? Could the alphabet be created by students?

- Are there photographs of your students in your room?

Hallways

What do visitors see when they walk into your school? At Green Gables Elementary, in Federal Way, Washington, couches, benches, and lamps are tucked into hallway niches. Checkerboards have been stenciled along the edges of the carpet, and bags with chess and checkers pieces hang nearby. These comfortable areas allow literacy activities to spill out into the hallways and invite parents, teachers, and students to stop and read, write, play games, or talk together. Families get the message that they are welcome to linger and participate in the school's literacy activities.

When visitors enter your building, do they immediately see student work that lets them know learning and students are the focus? Are the hallways welcoming, literacy rich, and inviting? The hallways in your home, your doctor's office, or the local museum are usually decorated with family photos, beautiful artwork, or photographs of local landscapes or other scenery. Hallways are places to display things we want to celebrate, ponder, enjoy, and discuss. You don't want artwork you don't appreciate or understand in your home; you want to decide what goes up on those walls. The same should be true in our schools. In too many schools, on the first of the month, a cluster of teaching assistants hang up commercial posters advocating healthy teeth, naming the body parts, or (if it's winter) depicting snowmen. (Some of them are a bit bedraggled, since they've been used for the last twenty-five years.) Instead, students should be encouraged to decorate the hallways with their artistic efforts and have a say about which learning artifacts from their classroom should be displayed.

At the American School in London, students' art is rotated frequently and is displayed in matted frames. The artwork is often accompanied by photographs of the artists at work, capturing both the final *product* and the creative

Ponder Box for Coaches and Principals

- Are the hallways of your school filled with students' reading and writing projects?

- Does the work on display reflect process as well as final products?

- Does the work on display reflect the unique population of your school?

process. Hallways become welcoming environments for literacy learning. The work we display and the areas we set up can capture student learning, invite collaboration, and create a beautiful, literacy-rich school.

Organizing Work Spaces, Desks, and Materials

Research in the last fifty years has shown that learning is a social and collaborative process and that students learn best when they are active and can talk about what they are learning. In *Still Learning to Read* (2003), Franki Sibberson and Karen Szymusiak note, "The way we set up our classroom gives our students a clear message about the culture of the classroom, the kind of work they will do, and the expectations we have for them" (29). The way you organize work spaces correlates directly with your beliefs about the social and collaborative nature of learning. A classroom with desks lined up in rows on a linoleum floor facing the teacher conveys a sense of regimentation and suggests a teacher-centered classroom. You can encourage conversation and collaboration by clustering four or five desks in groups or replacing desks with tables. You can also use these areas for small-group work, book clubs, writing response groups, and partnership conversations. You need to provide spaces to facilitate three different types of interactions that occur each day:

▶ Whole-class instruction

▶ Small-group instruction

▶ Independent work and individual conferences

Areas for Whole-Class Instruction

Students spend a great deal of time gathered for whole-class instruction, so it's important to create a cozy and inviting meeting space where all your students will fit comfortably and have room to turn and talk to one another about their thinking. These gatherings help build a sense of community. This space is most often defined by a rug; some teachers incorporate benches, bins, or crates along one side that provide both seating and storage.

Where do you sit for whole-class minilessons and read-alouds? Some of you may prefer a comfy overstuffed chair, while others like sitting in a rocking chair or perching on a bench or stool. You'll want to be able to make eye contact with students and have an easel, paper, and books handy. (This spot can often do double duty as the author's chair during writing workshop.) You should also have a basket or tub of markers, sticky notes, tape, sharpened pencils, and clipboards (or whiteboards and markers). The materials and spaces you provide should make your teaching easier.

Before and after writing/reading workshop, Sherri Ballew often gathers her fourth graders together at the front of the room for instruction. The area is big enough for everyone to fit, but still feels intimate and cozy. Students are separated from the distractions present at their desks or tables. At other times—when students share their work at the end of writing workshop, for example—she gathers her students in the library area; they form a circle so that everyone can make eye contact with one another. Being surrounded by books lets Sherri grab an example on the fly when she needs to.

Another consideration relative to the meeting area is how much foot traffic takes place there throughout the day. I once set up my meeting area right next to the classroom door, where students were coming and going throughout the day. On rainy or snowy days, students always scrambled for a "clean" spot away from the muddy footprints. I very quickly created another meeting area.

Sherri Ballew's Whole-Class Meeting Area

It's important to keep traffic patterns in mind as you design all the areas in your classroom. If you can prevent traffic jams, transitions between lessons are smoother and you'll have more time to teach.

Desks and Areas for Small-Group Instruction

You'll need to carve out at least one area in your room where you and your students can work together comfortably in a small group. Since your classroom is one in which you expect students to learn *with* one another, there should also be small nooks and crannies that the children know are designated spaces where they can work with one or two classmates. Melissa White

Cozy Nook in Melissa White and Karen Snyder's Classroom

and Karen Snyder have created a beautiful and inviting space under a "Peace" sign where students can curl up on pillows with a book.

Often when I visit Kate Morris's classroom, I have trouble spotting her. I'm most apt to discover her kneeling next to students at their desks or sitting cross-legged on the floor with a small group. She has one study carrel, which one student's IEP requires. This desk is also a good place for quiet conversations when the student isn't using it. If you don't have much space, you may want to set up a round table in the middle or side of your room for guided reading and small-group instruction. Let students know that the table is meant for small-group instruction but that if it's available, they can work at the table independently or with other students.

Anita Gallagher's Small-Group Meeting Area

In some classrooms, teachers substitute dining room tables, coffee tables, or end tables for traditional school desks in order to create a cozier environment. In her August 8, 2009, introductory letter to her weekly online newsletter, Brenda Power ruminates on Nancie Atwell's suggestion that classroom conversations should resemble the animated and friendly exchange of ideas that happens around the dining room table:

A few years ago Franki Sibberson realized there might be a literal truth in this ideal—if we bring real dining room tables into our classrooms and converse at them, the whole tenor of the conversations might change. Franki added a wooden table and chairs to her classroom seating arrangement, and immediately saw the quality of talk in conferences and small groups lift. I'm sure there are good scientific reasons that could be teased out to explain why and how dining room tables affect classroom talk. Here's my completely unscientific take. First, "coming to the table" promotes anticipation at home—of a meal, homework, shared tasks with people you love. Perhaps the background knowledge students bring to the task of "pulling up to the table" elevates their preparation a bit? Second, maybe there's a bunch of ultramodern homes in Beverly Hills that have dining room furniture made of metal and plastic. But for the most part, cold metal and plastic tables are only the norm in schools—not anywhere else. Wood is just warmer—it shows its scars and history proudly. There's a sense of traditions being born and carried on when you're sitting at an old table, at a time when it seems like so little in our world endures. If you want better conversations in your conferences with students, colleagues, or small groups this year, consider adding a "dining room style" table to your classroom or staff area. You can often find them at end-of-summer garage sales. You might be surprised at how quickly they can make your classroom feel more like home for students.

Some teachers provide clipboards for students who prefer to work seated on the floor or on pillows. I've seen a few classrooms with lofts or library nooks lined with pillows where children can snuggle up with books. Parents are often willing to donate furniture, make pillows, or build lofts, or you might be able to pick up the necessary materials at garage sales. Doriane Marvel has designed her classroom specifically to meet the needs of her students and to support instruction and describes how her classroom is arranged:

We use our carpet area to meet as a whole class. I can use chart paper or our classroom chalkboard. When I am using technology in a minilesson, the best position shifts to our desks so that everyone can see our dropdown screen or TV. For small-group work, we have two large tables. This allows students to work at one while I am instructing at another. There are many places to work, and depending on their mood and needs, students move about freely.

I love hearing or reading ideas that make me stop and say, "Wow, I've never thought of that." I had just this reaction when I read an article on the Choice Literacy website, "On Kidney Tables: Small Changes for Big Effects" (2006), in which Karen Szymusiak describes how sitting in the indentation of a kidney-shaped table made her think about the message she was giving her students. In order to convey a message of equality and a sense that she is also a learner, just like everyone else in the classroom, she replaced the kidney-shaped table in her classroom with a round table. What a perfect example of a "reflective practitioner" who thinks deeply about her classroom environment!

Areas for Independent Work and Individual Conferences

All of us know the value of having a private space in which we can work apart from the hustle and bustle of our surroundings. Because we expect our students to work independently at various times of the day, we need to provide the environment and the space that will allow them to do so successfully. Part of our responsibility is to make sure that we provide work areas in which the noise level is conducive to thinking. Some students may be able to do this in their designated classroom seat. Others may need an isolated place. Still others are able to work more comfortably curled on the floor with pillows or tucked into a rocking chair.

While the other children in the class are working independently, you're probably conferring with individual students. Some teachers prefer to confer with students *in situ*, right where they're working. Others, perhaps in part because of the room's configuration and lack of space between tables, decide to have students meet them at a designated conference table. Either way, students need room to spread out their work and enough quiet that they can be heard. You need to be able to make eye contact with the child and therefore need to be able to sit, kneel, or squat comfortably (the last two are getting harder for me the older I get!). Sherri Ballew sometimes conducts reading conferences at a table, while at other times she moves around the room to confer with students at their work tables. This one-on-one time is an opportunity for powerful teaching, and nearby students can benefit from it as they listen and sometimes chime in or offer advice.

Ponder Box for Teachers

● Do you have an area for whole-group instruction, preferably carpeted, with an easel, an overhead projector or document camera, clipboards, markers, and other writing materials handy?

● Is the meeting area comfortable and inviting?

● Have you considered your position in the room during minilessons in relation to your classroom door and to the flow of traffic in and out of your classroom?

● Do you have an area for small-group meetings, such as guided reading groups?

● Do students work at tables or clusters of desks?

● Is there a book area with pillows, a couch, and other comfortable places for kids to snuggle up and read?

● How will you accommodate the one or two students who may need absolute quiet and/or isolation when working independently?

● Do you have a quiet area for one-to-one conferences? Or is it more effective to engage in those conferences where other students can listen in?

● Do you have an area or two where individual students can work quietly?

The Teacher's Desk

When I went to elementary school, the visible symbol of the teacher's control over us, her students, was her imposing wooden desk, usually placed at the front of the classroom. The "silent message" was, *I'm in charge and I hold the most special place in this classroom*. Teachers spent most of their time writing at the blackboard, giving assignments, or sitting behind their desk, correcting papers, as we students worked silently, lined up alphabetically in rows of desks. I don't remember a teacher ever crouching down to talk to me about my work. Fortunately, that approach has been replaced by student-centered classrooms in which learning, rather than teaching, is the goal. Instead of sitting at your desk, you probably spend most of your time demonstrating literacy strategies at the whiteboard, creating anchor charts with the class, or conferring with students during independent work. Therefore, if you do have a desk, it might be time to ponder these questions: *What message does my desk convey? How often do I really use my desk? How much room does it take up? Where is the best place for my desk? Do I even need a desk?*

Sherri Ballew was so excited when she read *Spaces and Places* (2008), by Debbie Diller, and viewed *Simply Beautiful* (2006), by Gail Boushey and Joan Moser, that she totally rearranged her classroom. First, she eliminated her desk, which took up a lot of space. Once her desk was gone, she had more room for meeting areas and student desks, and her room felt more child centered. She used a filing cabinet to store most of her "teacher work" (the five drawers hold files for reading, writing, word work, math, science and social studies, as well as student information and test scores), and the metal sides made an excellent display area for magnetic poetry. She placed a round table, decorated with a plant and small lamp, next to the cabinet and students often work there during the day. After they go home, Sherri spreads out student work on the table as she grades, writes, or plans. Her computer is tucked in a space behind the table where she can easily turn to it and access files, websites, or her email.

Organizing Materials

As a writer, I understand the importance of having my space organized. Without this organization, I waste a lot of time searching for a file folder or a book I need. Sometimes when I can't find it, I have to rewrite whole passages. The work our students undertake in our classrooms is similar. My advice to teachers has always been, "The more time you put into thinking through and organizing your classroom, the more time you will have to *teach*!" The organization of materials in our classrooms can impede or enhance instruction. We want our classrooms to be neat and organized so that students can find the materials they need and work independently.

Once she removed her desk, Sherri Ballew had to reorganize her system for storing materials. In the back of the room, she now has stacking trays where students turn in their homework and other assignments. There is another table near the door where she keeps notes from the office, student reminders, and bathroom passes. She took home the professional books that she doesn't use every day and uses those five shelves for all her materials. The top shelf holds read-aloud novels and picture books that she knows she'll use for different units over the year. She also keeps a picture of her husband on the shelf, along with a little drawer for some extra whiteboard and colored markers. The next shelf down is positioned so that Sherri can write on it while standing up; it holds the phone, her plan book, a few professional books, a cup of pens, a pad of sticky notes, and her water bottle. The third shelf has two canvas boxes with handles that work like drawers. Those boxes hold rubber bands, paperclips, rubber stamps, and note cards. On the fourth shelf is a wire file holder with files labeled Monday through Friday in which she keeps papers for the week. That shelf is also where she stores her math curriculum books. The bottom shelf holds a few binders and a basket of books she is using for her current unit of study. Her document camera is connected to her computer that she has perched on a small table nearby.

Student materials are now stored in caddies at each table. Students keep all their reading and writing materials (their just-right chapter books, choice books, reading response journals, writer's notebooks, and word study notebooks) in color-coded book bins which cuts down on transition time, congestion, and clutter. Each table group also has a math basket that stores math journals, student reference books, geometry templates, and fact triangles. Students put these bins and baskets away when the materials are not in use. Sherri writes, "Keeping the classroom organized and teaching the kids how to keep it organized makes each day run smoother. I've had several former students return and comment on how open the room feels because of how I've rearranged it. Also, several parents have complimented me on how organized the room is."

Karen Snyder and Melissa White have also created cubbies in which students store their book boxes (filled with just-right books), their reading notebook (log, response sheets, strategy and conference forms), their portfolio, a tiny notebook with plastic sheets for poetry/songs introduced and read together, and their math journal. This helps keep their work tables clear of clutter and keeps the room neat.

When I taught in Colorado, I used one-third of my classroom for the block area, even in second grade. So much learning and creative play occurred as children constructed castles, cities, and imaginary worlds. The shelves were coded with laminated construction-paper shapes so students could put away the blocks on their own, and pencils and paper for making signs were at hand. It's disheartening to see fewer and fewer classrooms these days that contain shelves with those lovely wooden blocks. Even in early childhood classrooms, teachers have been pressured to reduce time spent allowing children to explore blocks, art techniques, and drama. In *Why Can't You Behave?* (2004), Paula Rogovin makes a plea for blocks and the arts, contending that they provide important opportunities for children to develop language, social skills, critical thinking, and creativity. In addition, these activities are fun—just listen to kindergartners giggle as they imitate adults in the play area or erect a zoo out of blocks. In Sheila Medow's Crow Island Elementary classroom, block building is a serious and creative activity. Sheila takes photographs of her students' constructions and displays pictures of buildings on the walls in the block area for inspiration. (See my website for photographs of Sheila's and Karen and Melissa's classrooms.)

Organizing Classroom Libraries

Much to my surprise, when I do walkthroughs in many schools, I see no class-room libraries. Children sometimes have copies of guided reading texts in their desks and some library books. This gives the clear message to children that they "own" no books of their own in the classroom and have to rely on the teacher to provide books from the school library or bookroom. How can chil-dren read independently every day unless they have books they can browse through and choose from in their own classroom? Without going into detail (I'm saving that for another book on reading instruction), let me just remind you that a classroom library is essential to a rich literacy program. Books are the bricks from which children build their foundation as readers and writers.

You'll need an overall organizational plan, including ways to store the books (shelves and baskets or tubs), category groupings (fiction, series, favorite authors, nonfiction content areas, fantasy, mysteries, favorite read-alouds, etc.), an area in which books are leveled by developmental stages so children can easily find the appropriate level of text, and ambient materials that create an inviting place to nestle in with a book (rugs, pillows, rocking chair, etc.). You can prepare all of this before school begins so that when the children walk into the room on the first day, they will be drawn to this invit-ing area of the classroom.

Once you have created your classroom library, children need an opportu-nity, within the first few weeks of school, to take on some of the ownership and responsibility of this important classroom space. Just as children can help you

Kathy Cullen's Classroom Library

create the materials that hang on your bulletin boards, they can take part in organizing the books in your classroom library. Hold a pile of books in reserve, explain the categories and organizational systems you've set up, and ask your students to help you place them where they belong. The conversations children have while making their decisions will give you instant information about their understanding of genres, text features, and overall book structure. So that they can continue to be responsible for the library throughout the year, present some recurring lessons on how to check out books, return books, find specific books, and locate "just-right" books (books matched to their independent reading levels) and materials that match their interests.

Creating Ambiance

We add little touches to make our homes special and welcoming places to work and relax. I have a collection of cobalt blue glass pieces on a window sash, magazines and current books on the coffee table, interesting items from my travels on the mantel, lots of green plants, and family photos in special frames. I have a comfortable chair in front of my computer (I spend a *lot* of time there) and my spot on the couch where I like to curl up with a book or watch TV. Without these special touches, my house could belong to anyone and wouldn't feel like my home. A similar ambience in a classroom sends the same message to our students. Since we spend so many hours every week at

Ambient Touches by Donna Hinton and Linda Lee

school with our students, why not make our classrooms feel as inviting, personal, and comfortable as our homes?

There are many little ways to add warmth and interest to your classroom. For instance, Megan Sloan places a lamp on a low table, along with a Curious George doll and a tub of books about that mischievous monkey. Linda Lee also uses lamps instead of the fluorescent lights in her classroom. Ranu Bhattacharyya has added a coffee table and couch to her classroom. A bead curtain makes a clever see-through area divider, and you can showcase new books on a stand on an end table. (Additional photographs of these classrooms may be found on my website, bonniecampbellhill.com.)

Ponder Box for Teachers

- How much time do you spend at your desk while children are in the classroom?

- How much room does your desk take up in your classroom?

- Do you need one large desk or would several small areas in your room work equally well?

- If you eliminated your desk, where would you store your materials, files, and books?

- Are there areas where you could add lamps, plants, or dividers?

- Could you add a couch, coffee table, or comfortable chairs?

- How could you add ambiance to your classroom?

- Do you have storage areas for materials for reading, writing, math, and content areas?

- Do students have book boxes or a place to keep the books they're currently reading?

- Do you have a system for organizing and maintaining the pencils/markers, papers, books, and materials that students use daily?

- Do you have a classroom library? Have you focused on how to organize it to support students' independent reading?

- How will you maintain your organization and management system once it is designed?

- Where do you store your professional books and materials?

Creating and Displaying Anchor Charts

If someone walked into your classroom, could they tell what minilessons you have presented this week? Are the same tattered charts thumb-tacked to the bulletin board in September still there in May? Can visitors see evidence of students' learning about your current unit of study? Nancy Akhavan (2004) states, "By looking at the charts, I felt I could see the wheels of learning whiz around inside the children's heads" (37).

Creating inviting, literacy-rich classrooms is not just about lovely bulletin boards and cozy book areas. It's also about content. How do your walls reflect your latest teaching and your students' learning? As part of the gradual release of responsibility approach (Pearson and Gallagher 1983) of teaching and learning, you will conduct lots of minilessons in which you model your own reading and writing process. You will introduce strategies that readers and writers use or the characteristics of a specific genre you are studying. In order for students to be a part of this process, record their thoughts on chart paper. An anchor chart is a handwritten poster or graphic representation that serves as a visual reminder of strategies, ideas, or vocabulary that students are learning. It is a reference tool that "anchors" new and ongoing learning to key concepts they learned previously. Students are expected to refer to the anchor charts as they incorporate new strategies or concepts in their independent work. These anchor charts then become a part of your classroom learning environment, and you can refer back to them during other minilessons and add to these charts over time. Anchor charts are scaffolds that lead students to use strategies and information independently. By recording students' thinking, you are making learning both public and permanent.

When I visited in October, Sherri Ballew's classroom was already so full of minilesson charts that she had to clamp ones from earlier in the year on a pants hanger! Walking around her classroom, I saw that she had been talking with her students about comprehension strategies. Reading Sherri's neatly printed charts, I could tell she had read *Strategies That Work* (2007) by Stephanie Harvey and Anne Goudvis, and incorporated their tips for teaching comprehension strategies. I could see from another chart that she had been showing her

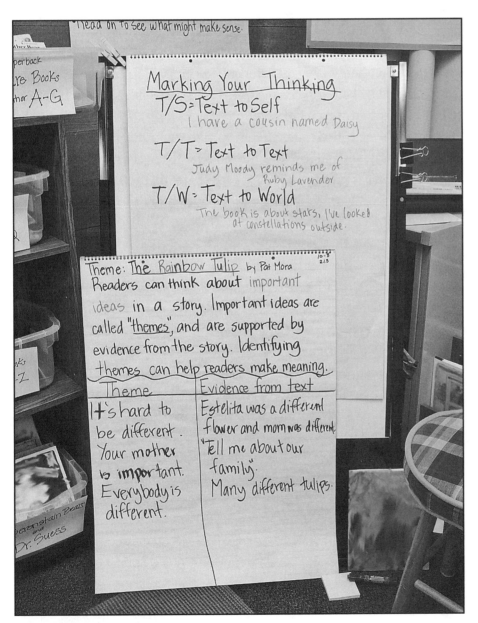

Sherri Ballew's Anchor Charts

fourth graders how to use sticky notes to mark where they made text-to-text, text-to-world, and text-to-self connections. Still another chart summarized her minilesson about theme and how to provide evidence from a text. The day I observed her classroom, Sherri pointed to the charts several times, and I saw students read and refer to them as well. Anchor charts, when created collaboratively and displayed publically, dramatically support students as they internalize all those tips, strategies, and insights that you've discovered together.

Sherri doesn't spend her classroom budget on commercial posters about writing or reading, nor does she create her charts in her best teacher handwriting at home before teaching a lesson. These charts are rich because they were created *with* her students *in* the classroom. Sherri's students are more likely to refer back to her lessons, because their voices boom from those charts. Anchor charts are only valuable if students use them as support during group work and independent reading and writing. Sherri mentioned that since she's started using a document camera, she thinks carefully about when to project her writing, her students' writing, or pages from books and when it would be better to create an anchor chart. Since space in her classroom is limited, at the end of each unit, Sherri collects the charts, takes a photo of each one with her digital camera, and stores the photos in a picture album. This way, she and her students can refer to the charts throughout the year, and she saves precious wall space for charts that reflect new learning.

Teacher Eliza Lewis has this to say about creating anchor charts:

I consider charting an organic process in my classroom. Anything charted comes directly from an experience that those students and I have had together. The charts in my classroom can be wildly different from year to year, based on kids' needs, how the series of lessons developed, the language that I stole from the kids, and what I need to emphasize with each group of students.

Often our charts will begin with some notes or a web roughed out on the classroom whiteboard. The students and I move ideas around and fine-tune until I think we have something worth saving—something that will serve both as a reminder of what we have learned and done and as a guide for what students can now do independently. My students use the charts a lot, because they co-create them with me and the charts support their growing competencies.

To me, charts are far more than mere decorations. The only reason to chart with kids is so that students have something to hold onto as they work independently—and kids use the charts that they help create.

As an alternative to taking photos of anchor charts they've created with their students as references for independent work, some teachers put typed versions in labeled pockets on a bulletin board for students to refer to as needed. Literacy coach Mimi Brown stores her charts in legal-sized manila envelopes. She writes the topic on the outside of the folder and stands the envelopes up in a box covered with contact paper.

Some teachers use an interactive whiteboard (IWB) to record their minilessons. While IWBs are very effective for showing video clips and accomplishing interactive tasks, I worry that the "footprint" or written evidence of a minilesson will be lost and that students won't be able to refer to visual reminders of the lesson. At one school, the teachers worked so hard at crafting their lessons for each unit of study that they decided to record them permanently on their interactive whiteboards. When I asked how the students would be able to refer back to the charts as they were working on their writing projects, the answer was, "They'd just ask me and I'd quickly flip through the charts stored on my computer." Rather than referring to the charts independently, students would have to ask for the teacher's help, probably while the teacher was conducting a conference with another student. The purpose of charts is to scaffold the students' learning while they are working independently so that

Ponder Box for Teachers

- Do the charts displayed throughout your classroom reflect your most recent minilessons?
- Do students refer to the charts throughout the day?
- Where do you store charts from previous lessons or units?

Ponder Box for Coaches and Principals

- Do you see anchor charts in most classrooms in your school?
- Do the anchor charts change to reflect teachers' current units and minilessons?
- How can you support the use of anchor charts throughout the school?

eventually they will internalize the strategies. If you do use an IWB, I urge you either to still use paper anchor charts or to print out the information on the charts and tuck these pages in envelopes on a bulletin board or into a notebook so that students can refer to these tips independently. Anchor charts should reflect and guide your teaching but also help your students use literacy strategies on their own.

Evaluating Your Classroom Environment

One of my goals for this chapter is to enable you to evaluate your own classroom by showcasing classrooms that support literacy learning. Many elements in these examples are probably already reflected in your own classroom. Other elements may inspire you to make changes that will improve your teaching and learning. I hope you have come to see all the classroom teachers I've described and published authors I've quoted as encouraging colleagues willing to share ideas.

You also have experts in your own professional backyard. Some of the teachers at your school have created inviting areas for whole-class and small-group learning, as well as areas for conferring and working with individual students. Some have bravely removed their desks and created innovative ways to store materials and supplies. A few have added delightful and creative touches to enhance the ambience of their classrooms. But how will you know about these exciting innovations?

Even if your best friend teaches down the hall, you may rarely have a chance to visit his or her classroom. During my classroom walkthroughs before school workshops, principals who take me from class to class often remark on how much they notice during these visits. Classroom teachers rarely get this opportunity. Most teachers are caught up in the world of their own classroom and grab every free minute to read or display student work, email parents, find the perfect book for a minilesson, or plan for the next day. One simple way to open up the doors between classrooms is to conduct faculty meetings, grade-level meetings, or book studies in a different classroom each week.

Teachers spent a staff meeting in Barbara Coleman's North Carolina classroom discussing classroom environments (Choice Literacy website, "Classroom Tours," 2007), after which trios of mixed-grade teachers (including specialists) walked through the school. Each group of three teachers visited three classrooms, using a set of questions to focus their observations. When possible the classroom teacher was the "tour guide," someone else asked the questions, and the remaining member of the group recorded the answers.

When the staff reconvened forty-five minutes later, two sets of trios met and shared their observations and the new ideas they had encountered that they might incorporate in their own classrooms. Barbara writes, "We believe we saw far more change, more quickly, than if we had tried to mandate or require specific environmental changes. . . . It was an hour of staff time well spent."

If you conduct walkthroughs as a staff, you may want to focus on particular aspects of the classroom. For instance, if it's "The Year of the Writer" at your school, teachers may want to observe how student work is displayed in various classrooms. (There's also a wonderful checklist on pages 48 and 49 of Katie Wood Ray's *The Writing Workshop* [2001] that lists the things she looks for when she visits a writing workshop classroom.) If your staff is focusing on reading, you may want to share ideas about how books are organized and displayed in classroom libraries.

When our family visits our southern relatives, the inevitable comment to my kids is always, "My, how you've grown." This isn't surprising, since it's usually been four or five years since we visited. When they last saw Bruce he was a shy, skinny, eighth grader with braces and glasses. Now he's a six-foot, straight-toothed, contact-lens–wearing college freshman they can hardly recognize. They can't help but remark on the change, which isn't nearly as dramatic to me since I see him every day. In the same way, it's sometimes hard for

Book List

Resources for Creating Beautiful and Inviting Classrooms

- [ ] *Spaces and Places* by Debbie Diller (2008) (K–5)

- [ ] *Teaching with Intention* by Debbie Miller (Chapter 3) (2008) (K–5)

- [ ] *Classroom Management in Photographs* by Maria Chang (2004) (K–5)

- [ ] *Simply Beautiful* by Gail Boushey and Joan Moser (DVD) (2006) (K–5)

- [ ] *Classroom Spaces That Work* by Marlynn Clayton and Mary Beth Forton (2003) (K–5)

- [ ] *Classroom Management* by Irene Fountas and Gay Su Pinnell (DVD) (2005) (K–3) teachers (and students) to see the changes in their classroom environments. That's why it's important to keep a journal and take pictures so you can celebrate how much you've grown. The Classroom Environment and Community of Learners rubric can also help you document growth and changes.

Ponder Box for Teachers

- Where would you place yourself on the Classroom Environment and Hallways row of the rubric that follows?

- Have you visited other teachers' classrooms?

- Would you be willing to invite your colleagues to visit your classroom?

- Which professional books and videos or DVDs would you like to explore on this topic?

Ponder Box for Coaches and Principals

- Where is your school on the Classroom Environment and Hallways row of the rubric that follows?

- What do you see as "next steps" for teachers in this area?

- Could you conduct staff meetings, book studies, or grade-level meetings in different classrooms?

- Would teachers like to meet in groups of three to share ideas about classroom environments?

- Could the literacy coach develop a protocol for classroom visits?

- Could the literacy coach set up a model classroom in your building?

- How can you support inquiry on this topic in a few classrooms, at grade levels, or in the whole school? (classroom visitations? book studies? articles?)

- Would teachers like the chance to read some professional books or watch some videos or DVDs about classroom environment as an interest group, a grade level, or as a K–5 faculty?

Classroom Environment and Community of Learners (Teacher Rubric)

NOVICE	APPRENTICE	PRACTITIONER	LEADER
		Classroom	
☐ Desks are arranged in rows; I have created or purchased most of the material on the walls/bulletin boards; the student work displayed is mostly homogeneous	☐ There are a few areas for group work; I have created or purchased some material for the walls/bulletin boards, some student-created work is displayed	☐ Tables or desks are arranged for small-group work; there is a comfortable area for whole-class meetings; walls/bulletin boards are filled with varied examples of student work and class-generated charts summarizing minilessons	☐ Comfortable, inviting areas have been specifically designed for whole-group, small-group, and individual work; tables or desks are arranged for small-group work; walls/bulletin boards are filled with displays of student work, environmental print, and class-generated charts that change over time and reflect student reading and writing, inquiry, and the learning process; students consistently refer to the charts as they work

Classroom Environment and Community of Learners (School Rubric)

NOVICE	APPRENTICE	PRACTITIONER	LEADER
		Classrooms and Hallways	
☐ In most classrooms, desks are arranged in rows; bulletin boards, walls and hallways contain mostly teacher-created or purchased materials; some homogeneous student work is displayed	☐ In most classrooms, there are a few areas for group work; bulletin boards, walls and hallways contain some teacher-created or purchased materials; some student-created work is displayed	☐ In most classrooms, tables or desks are arranged for small-group work; in most classrooms, there are comfortable areas for whole-class meetings; in most classrooms, walls/bulletin boards are filled with varied examples of student work and class-generated charts summarizing mini-lessons	☐ In all classrooms, comfortable, inviting areas have been designed for whole-group, small-group, and individual work; in all classrooms, tables or desks are arranged for small-group work; walls/bulletin boards and hallways are filled with displays of student work, environmental print, and class-generated charts that change over time and reflect student reading and writing, inquiry, and the learning process; in all classrooms, students often refer to the charts as they work

2

Forming a Community

The social aspects of your classroom that support learning are even more vital than the physical environment. Students need to feel valued and appreciated before they are ready to learn, take risks, trust others, and feel part of the classroom community of learners. This chapter explores three specific challenges that arise in classrooms:

- ▶ cultural differences
- ▶ linguistic differences
- ▶ learning differences

Establishing a Culturally Responsive Classroom

How many of your students come from other countries and backgrounds? How do you acknowledge the various cultures represented in your school? In 1960, 15 percent of the population was composed of minorities. In 2005, that number climbed to 33 percent. According to a 2008 Pew Research Center report, the percentage of non-Caucasians in this country is expected to reach 53 percent by the year 2050, in which case the "minority" will become the majority (Passel and Cohn 2008). Our schools are becoming more and more diverse.

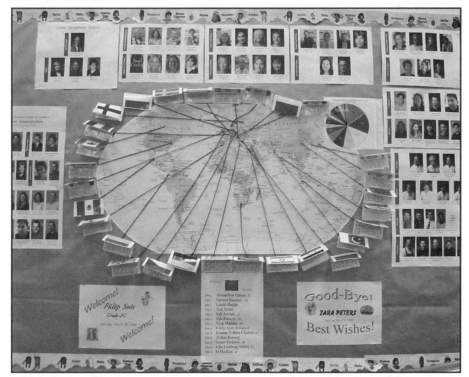

Bulletin Boards at the American International School of Budapest Value Cultural Diversity

In many schools, the major forms of cultural appreciation are the annual potluck with foods from representative countries and celebrations of Hanukkah, Kwanza, and the Chinese New Year. In *Beneath the Surface* (2008), Ken Pransky calls these differences in religion, music, and food the "tip of the cultural iceberg" (4). He claims that students appreciate seeing aspects of their culture valued and that this is the first step toward creating a culturally responsive classroom and school.

A teacher at the International School of Budapest welcomes students with a bulletin board on which she has written *hello* in all the languages her students speak. A bulletin board including all the teachers' names, photographs, and nationalities is posted in the front hallway.

The Manhattan New School also has students from many countries around the world. In *Writing Through Childhood* (2001), Shelley Harwayne describes how she heard several students who had recently moved to New York talking about missing their homelands. With her support, the students wrote and posted "manuscript wanted" signs and created an anthology in a three-ring binder about the challenges of moving to a new country.

These are a few of many ways in which we can acknowledge how hard it is to move to a new country and learn a new language and to let students know that we value the richness that their varied backgrounds bring to our classrooms and schools.

However, Ken Pransky says that other, more significant factors form the hidden layers of the "cultural iceberg." These involve different ways of thinking, feeling, believing, valuing, acting, and using language that stem from differences of class, race, dialect, and register (2008, 3–5). Even our gestures and body language can provide challenges for some students. Cheryl Perkins tells a story about taking her students to their first assembly. She carefully prepared the first graders by discussing correct behavior and explaining how they all had to sit "criss-cross applesauce" on the floor so that the children behind them could see. Cheryl mentioned that she would be at the end of the row and would give a signal (first two fingers crossed) as a reminder if anyone forgot to sit flat. One little boy had a horrified expression on his face. Cheryl later learned that in Cambodia, that hand gesture is incredibly rude and suggestive. No wonder the little boy was baffled and a little shocked!

In *One Classroom, Many Worlds* (2003), Jacklyn Blake Clayton explores both differences among cultures that are observable (such as customs and traditions) and other, more hidden differences (ways of thinking and acting) that are based on our upbringing and social context. For example, when you were growing up, what was the criterion for being a "good boy" or "good girl"? How was your socialization different from that of your parents or grandparents? Jacklyn includes a thought-provoking continuum about family orientation and child-rearing values that will prompt interesting discussions at a staff meeting. How much do you know about differences in verbal and nonverbal communication and differences between various cultures? (For example, the way many Americans signal "come" with the palm up and one finger beckoning is considered an insulting gesture in other cultures.) In her book, Jacklyn explains differences between cultures in the amount of eye contact and touching, the size of people's personal space, patterns of lining up, and even the way people smile. The more aware we are of these differences, the more appreciation and understanding we can have of our culturally and linguistically diverse students.

In international schools, the challenges of honoring varying cultures can be overwhelming, because many classrooms have students from at least ten different cultures. Some classrooms in the United States are equally diverse. We want to help students feel comfortable in our classrooms; however, we also need to empower students to hold on to their own cultural values as they become part of an English-speaking community. This can be a tricky balancing act for our students and their families. We need to be patient as we work to establish a responsive classroom.

Some parents go to extraordinary lengths to make sure their children succeed in school, bending over backward so that they'll "fit in." For example, some Korean families ask their children to drop their Korean names in favor of an American-style name at school. Recently I visited a third-grade classroom where I read *The Name Jar* (2003) by Yangsook Choi, aloud. In the story, a young Asian girl has come to an American school and is trying to decide what her American name will be. Her classmates become involved, and one of them coyly convinces the girl to keep her Asian name because it is so special. As I was reading the text, two Korean boys were whispering to one another. Then one of them said in a soft voice, "That's me." Because I was an outsider with no background in the classroom, I turned to the teacher who explained, with tears in her eyes, that the students in this class had tried to convince this young boy to keep his Korean name, but he had decided to take the name Paul. We talked briefly about the way the class and especially the teacher had been willing to try to learn how to say his Korean name, but that he just wanted to make the change. His parents had encouraged their son to retain his Korean name at school, but left the decision up to him.

The next day I returned to this classroom for another demonstration lesson with a new book to read aloud. "Paul" was very attentive and kept smiling at me. As soon as the students began reading independently, the teacher pulled me over to her desk and showed me "Paul's" math test on which he had erased his American name and had written his Korean name in its place. She had asked him privately which name he would like to use, and he said he wanted to use his Korean name "just like the girl in the story."

The teacher and I rejoiced in the positive effect of her efforts to support all children and their cultures and the ability of a story or children's book to spark conversations like this.

Other books about names and culture are *My Name Is Jorge: On Both Sides of the River* (2004), by Jane Medina, *My Name Was Hussein* (2004), by Hristo Kyuchukov, and *My Name Is Yoon* (2003), by Helen Recorvits. In her article entitled "Honoring Children's Names and, Therefore, Their Identities," Mariana Souto-Manning (2007) comments that "by recognizing the importance of names, communicating that importance to parents, and honoring names in schools, teachers can give children access to classroom communities while broadening everyone's worldviews. Recognizing and valuing diverse cultures and identities then becomes fundamental to forming true classroom communities" (2). Jacklyn Clayton (2003) writes, "Multiculturalism reaches across not just racial, cultural, or ethnic groups, but also across gender, age, and disability. Multiculturalism means an awareness of all these various groups with their differing patterns of behavior, but it also reaches beyond the *what* of those differences to investigate the *why*. Multiculturalism means being proud of the cultural diversity of this country" (170). We need to move beyond tolerance to an affirmation of differences. If students feel their cultures are valued and appreciated, they will become eager participants and learners in our classrooms.

Book List

Resources for Helping You Create Culturally Responsive Classrooms

☐ *Beneath the Surface* by Ken Pransky (2008) (K–6)

☐ *One Classroom, Many Worlds* by Jacklyn Blake Clayton (2003) (K–5)

☐ *Building Culturally Responsive Classrooms* by Concha Delgado Gaitan (2006) (K–6)

☐ *Divided We Fail* by Crystal England (2008) (K–12)

☐ *Classroom Diversity* by Ellen McIntyre, Ann Rosebery, and Norma Gonzales (2001) (K–5)

☐ *Teaching Fairly in an Unfair World* by Kathleen Lundy (2008) (K–12)

In *Beneath the Surface* (2008), Ken Pransky explores the impact of students' home language, culture, and socioeconomic status on student learning. He claims that student learning is also influenced by whether their families are *literacy oriented*. He urges teachers to be cautious about stereotyping and deficit thinking in order to provide support for all our students. Our goal should be to build positive relationships with all our students and their families by demonstrating that we value their home experiences, cultures, and languages and by being advocates for families of all students.

Ponder Box for Teachers

- How culturally responsive is your classroom?

- Did any of the strategies mentioned in this chapter pique your interest in reading any of the professional books to learn more strategies to make your classroom more culturally responsive?

- How can you learn more about the various cultures of your students?

- What are some ways you could honor the various cultures and languages represented in your classroom?

Ponder Box for Coaches and Principals

- How culturally respectful and responsive is your school?

- Might you offer the teachers the chance to read some professional books or watch some videos or DVDs about cultural awareness as an interest group, a grade-level focus, or a faculty?

- Which resources would be most helpful?

- Do the ESL/ELL teachers have tips about this topic to share with the rest of the staff?

Modifying the Classroom Environment for English Language Learners

How many languages are spoken in your classroom? Do you have any students who speak virtually no English? Spending their days in a classroom in which they only understand a few words can be both overwhelming and exhausting for these students. Yet by the end of the year, most of them are shouting on the playground and chiming in during songs, have made friends, and are well on their way to becoming fluent English speakers. There are ways in which we can ease the stress and provide a welcoming social environment for students who are immersed in a new language. *English Learners in American Classrooms* (2007), by James Crawford and Stephen Krashen, and *Working with English Language Learners* (2007), by Stephen Cary, answer almost any questions you might have about working with ELLs.

When I taught in Colorado, the majority of the students in my classroom were not native English speakers, and a huge range of factors affected how quickly they learned English. Mike was from New Zealand, and apart from his charming accent, the challenges of school in the United States were minimal. Tanya moved to Colorado from Serbia; her parents spoke fluent English, and she already knew how to read in her native language. I remember vividly Tanya reading *One Fish, Two Fish, Red Fish, Blue Fish* (1960) by Dr. Seuss aloud to me in October in her lovely Eastern European accent and moaning, "This is so *dumb!*" She was speaking, reading, and writing fluently in English by the end of December. Thai was a Cambodian refugee. He had never been to school, didn't know his age, had not learned to read in his native language, had never even worn shoes, and carried with him the trauma of living in refugee camps and seeing family members killed. His journey (in school and in life) was filled with many hurdles and challenges.

To meet the needs of *all* your students, you need to create a *social context* in which your English language learners (ELLs) can flourish. I can only dip my toe into the topic here, but ways in which you can improve your classroom environment for ELLs include:

▶ Create a bulletin board that lists all your students' names and the languages they speak.

▶ Learn how to correctly pronounce the names of all your students and learn a few phrases in each child's language.

▶ Research their cultural background in the library or on the Internet.

▶ Get to know their hobbies and interests.

- Display photographs and books that represent their home countries.

- Make an extra effort to connect with their families.

- Create a welcoming and risk-taking environment.

- Celebrate each child's strengths.

- Level the playing field with art.

- Allow students to process information and talk in their first language.

- Pair them with partners who are accepting and supportive.

- Explicitly teach important phrases in English.

- Model respect and acceptance of differences.

- Arrange furniture so that students can socialize and collaborate.

- Label materials using rebuses or pictures.

- Model procedures and classroom routines.

As you set up your classroom, you will also want to consider how to modify the *physical* environment to support the needs of your ELLs. The first chapter in *English Language Learners Day by Day K–6* (2009) by Christina Celic describes how you can provide support by considering your classroom layout, classroom library selection (including leveled books in students' first language), literacy charts, and materials.

It's also important to read some professional books about meeting the needs of ELLs. As a new principal last year at a bilingual school on the Mexican border, Sandi Figueroa purchased a copy of *Balanced Literacy for English Language Learners, K–2* (2006), by Linda Chen and Eugenia Mora-Flores, for all her primary teachers. During their summer literacy institute, the teachers used the book to plan their daily instruction for the year, and they continued to use it for support when they began following the plan. It provided a strong foundation of knowledge and a common language as Sandi and her colleagues wrestled with how to better support the ELLs in their school and classrooms. By the end of the year, the teachers had a strong grasp of second language acquisition and classroom practices. They understood that literacy development is a lifelong process of creating meaning from one's environment. They realized that they needed to be very intentional about their instruction but also to create a classroom environment that supports ELLs.

In their booklet *A Quick Guide to Boosting English Acquisition* (2008), Alison Porcelli and Cheryl Tyler describe the framework for their "choice workshop," a daily time in which the children interact socially while Alison and Cheryl confer with them and explicitly teach skills and strategies. The workshop has a structure similar to reading/writing workshop: a five-minute minilesson, twenty-five to thirty-five minutes spent working independently, and five minutes for "teaching shares." Alison and Cheryl present between four and six choice workshop units of study that complement their units of study for reading/writing workshop in their primary classrooms. Alison and Cheryl believe that all children need opportunities to work with blocks, experiment with art materials, and participate in dramatic play. It's even more important for ELLs, because the social interactions and concrete materials provide the support they need to communicate and strengthen their vocabulary.

Nancy Akhavan has a slightly different take on providing a context in which students new to English can learn and practice language skills. In her book *Help! My Kids Don't All Speak English* (2006), Nancy describes in specific detail how a daily thirty-minute language workshop (in addition to a reading and writing workshop) can help close the achievement gap for

Fiona Sheridan conducts a Parent Workshop for Families of English Language Learners at the International School of Beijing

ELLs. Her language workshop begins with a minilesson (five or ten minutes), followed by guided practice (twenty or thirty minutes) in which students talk or write about a text Nancy reads aloud, followed by quick sharing and a wrap-up.

It's especially important to provide a risk-free environment for ELLs. In *Classroom Instruction That Works with English Language Learners* (2006), Jane Hill and Kathleen Flynn suggest that the two questions that worry ELLs most are, *Will this teacher like me?* and *Can I do the work?* They need to know that we accept their initial errors in grammar and pronunciation as part of the

Book List

Resources for Helping You Modify Your Classroom for ELLs

☐ *Balanced Literacy for English Language Learners* by Linda Chen and Eugenia Mora-Flores (2006) (K–2)

☐ *Classroom Instruction That Works* by Jane Hill and Kathleen Flynn (2006) (K–8)

☐ *A Quick Guide to Boosting English Acquisition* by Alison Porcelli and Cheryl Tyler (2008) (K–2)

☐ *English Learners in American Classrooms* by James Crawford and Stephen Krashen (2007) (K–12)

☐ *Working with English Language Learners* by Stephen Cary (2007) (K–12)

☐ *Help! My Kids Don't All Speak English* by Nancy Akhavan (2006) (K–8)

☐ *A How-To Guide for Teaching English Language Learners in the Primary Classroom* by Pat Barrett Dragan (2005) (K–2)

☐ *"The Words Came Down!" English Language Learners Read, Write, and Talk Across the Curriculum* by Emelie Parker and Tess Pardini (2006) (K–2)

☐ *Beneath the Surface* by Ken Pransky (2008) (K–6)

☐ *Making Content Comprehensible for English Learners* by Jana Echevarria, MaryEllen Vogt, and Deborah Short (2009) (K–8)

☐ *English Language Learners Day by Day* by Christina Celic (2009) (K–6)

process of learning a new language. They write, "The best way for you, as a teacher, to deal with them is to model correct structures by unceremoniously restating what students say. Overly correcting grammar and pronunciation can generate anxiety, which in turn can inhibit natural language acquisition" (35).

You can also support students by respecting and honoring their first language. Pat Barrett Dragan, in *A How-To Guide for Teaching English Language Learners in the Primary Classroom* (2005), creates this sort of welcoming environment by greeting each student by name on the first day of school and (using "cheat sheets" she's posted on the walls) welcoming them and their families in their home languages. She fills her classroom with books and photos from the countries represented so all children will feel welcome. Pat gets to know her students through their self-portraits and autobiographies and in individual interviews. She uses the library and Internet to research the cultural backgrounds of her students. She writes, "One of my main goals is to create a classroom climate that is low on anxiety and high on zest for learning" (23).

Parent workshops are held at the International School of Beijing on a regular basis on Thursday from 8:30–10:30. Because English is not the first language for many of their students, the teachers hold a parent workshop about language acquisition early in the year, emphasizing the importance of maintaining a strong mother tongue. They provide a small booklet with the principles of language acquisition and create a display which is posted in the hallway. In addition to conferences with classroom teachers, ELL teachers also hold brief ten-minute conferences at the beginning of the year in which parents share their hopes and fears for their child. As you strive to educate and

Ponder Box for Teachers

- How many students in your classroom are officially labeled ELLs?

- How many students are not receiving special services but are still not as fluent in academic English as native English speakers?

- How many languages are spoken in your classroom?

- How often and how well do you communicate with the ESL/ELL teacher?

- What are some ways you could honor the various cultures and languages represented in your classroom?

Ponder Box for Coaches and Principals

- How many students in your school are officially labeled ELLs?

- How many students are not receiving special services but are still not as fluent in academic English as native English speakers?

- How many languages are spoken at your school?

- Are materials for families translated into those languages?

- Might you offer teachers the chance to read some professional books or watch some videos or DVDs about working with ELLs as an interest group, a grade-level focus, or a faculty?

- Do ESL/ELL teachers have tips about this topic to share with the rest of the staff?

involve your ELL parents, you may want to weave some research, quotes, and suggestions from some of the resources in the booklist in parent newsletters and workshop.

Differentiating Learning for All Students

When I was a brand-new teacher, I had some very wonderful but sometimes challenging students. The first language for the majority of them was not English. I also had a range of students with other needs. That first year, one student set the bathroom on fire and another waylaid students in the hallway and demanded their lunch money. I had a student with a hearing impairment and one with leg braces. I asked for support from the reading teacher, the special education teacher, and the psychologist. After many months, they offered a diagnosis and a label for these worrisome students but never suggested what I could do differently to meet their needs. Throughout the year, I found I needed to modify my instruction based on my students' needs, interests, and backgrounds. By the end of the year, my ELLs were speaking English fluently and the behavioral challenges had diminished—we were a community of learners—but it was a year I will never forget!

In today's budget-minded economy, many services for at-risk students are being cut or discontinued even as our classrooms are filled with more and more kids who face challenges at home, have learning disabilities, or learn in different ways. The simultaneous mania for high-stakes testing and accountability puts pressure on students with cultural, linguistic, and learning differences to meet the same standards and pass the same tests as their classmates. Understanding differentiation and inclusion can help you develop the necessary community of learners that will make your classroom welcoming and successful for all your students.

Differentiation

How do you modify the social aspects of your classroom to meet the needs of individual learners? Do you group students by need or by ability? Are groups permanent or flexible? Research in the past ten years has shown ability grouping to be ineffective in meeting children's individual needs. Some other negative impacts of grouping are the stigma attached to being in the low group, the different social status of students in high and low groups, different expectations for achievement (on the part of both pupils and teachers), and the difficulty of moving out of a group once placed there. Yet ability grouping, especially for reading, remains a common practice in many schools.

In the Introduction, I described a school that tracked students by reading levels. The principal and some of the teachers realized that some children, especially the ones who were struggling, were not developing adequate reading skills. They suspected that part of the problem was the lack of small-group instruction, individual conferences, and independent reading

The school had used ability grouping for over twelve years. Teachers were not encouraged to investigate current best practices; very few teachers attended workshops or read books on the latest teaching methods. After my initial visit, Carrie worked with the staff and introduced the concept of heterogeneous instruction within a workshop format. A core group of teachers began implementing these changes and immediately saw the effect of differentiation on student learning. Eventually, the school's administration adopted a plan for all teachers to implement workshop instruction within two years. The school provided onsite coaching and set aside time for teacher teams to collaborate. Over the course of a few visits by Carrie, more and more teachers became convinced of the positive benefits of differentiated instruction on the culture of their classrooms. Teachers have now embraced workshop instruction, are reading professional books, and sharing ideas. Classroom libraries are filled with a variety of texts. This revitalization was made possible by taking that first step away from whole-group instruction and ability grouping.

Kerry Harder leads a Differentiation Workshop at the International School of Muscat

The teachers at The American International School of Muscat (Oman) in the Middle East had varied interpretations of the term *differentiation*. Many of them were using aspects of differentiated instruction but not recognizing them as such. Others wanted to know more and expand their practice in this area. The teaching and learning committee wanted to establish a common definition; recognize the many types and purposes for differentiating instruction; and begin purposeful, intentional planning for differentiation.

To that end, the student services coordinator, ELL coordinator, and literacy coordinator planned and led a workshop for the entire staff (including specialists, assistants, and secretaries) in which they shared differentiation activities that were already being used in classrooms. Participants were divided into three groups. Each group read different articles about differentiation by Carol Tomlinson, summarized them, and shared significant concepts with the whole group. The staff then designed a poster stating what they wanted differentiation to look like at their school and used this vision to guide their literacy instruction. They are now transferring those same concepts about differentiation into their mathematics program.

For these teachers, differentiation is not only important in their classroom instruction but also a critical part of their classroom environment. Giving children many opportunities throughout the day to work in a variety of instructional settings—with a partner, in small and large groups, individually—mirrors life outside school. Imagine only ever associating with the same like-minded group at work! The cross-pollination triggered as different individuals and different groups of people work together and listen to different ideas and perspectives would never take place. The same is true for your students. Their lives are enriched though social interactions with peers who have different personalities, interests, and abilities.

The story of these two schools highlights how grouping practices can be modified to address the needs of students. Grouping and similar aspects of differentiation can be figured out in advance. For instance, if you have a student who has trouble concentrating, you may need to create a quiet work area or seat that child close to you during minilessons. Other decisions are made on the spot, based on what happens that day and what you know about each learner. For example, you may decide to allow two students more time or more support during a nonfiction research project.

Here's a story from my own classroom. Ray knew he was not as strong a reader as many of his buddies. He needed instruction in a small group with similar readers. But he *begged* me to let him read *Little Bear* (Minarik 1978) along with some of his friends, even though he and I both knew the book was beyond his ability at the time. He worked with his friends in large groups and partnerships in content areas throughout the day, but he also wanted to read this special book with them. We carved out five minutes every day when he and his friend Thomas could read this book together. Watching them focus intently on reading the book and listening to their conversation about it, I knew this one small change had afforded a powerful learning opportunity to both boys. Thomas was using his reading strategies to coach his friend. Ray was working harder than ever to read the one book he wanted to read and clearly delighted in the chance to talk about it. I realized then how important it is to differentiate learning to match the social as well as the instructional needs of our students.

Responsive teaching is an essential component of reading/writing workshop. It enables you to meet the needs of *all* your students and make them feel they are valued members of the community. You can provide materials that match each child's needs, learning styles, interests, and strengths. In reading workshop, you can help students select just-right books. During writing workshop, you can vary your expectations for length, complexity, and amount of revision. The factors in your classroom environment you can modify to differentiate your instruction include:

- grouping practices
- texts and materials
- physical environment

amount of support and expectations

 time

In *The Differentiated School* (2008), Carol Ann Tomlinson and her colleagues point out that differentiation is not an extra topic but a lens through which we can view instruction in order to teach responsively. This can best be done by collecting data about your students, then modifying your curriculum and instruction to meet the needs of your diverse learners. The most significant outcome of one elementary school's journey toward differentiation was that "teachers began seeing students as the engine that drives the teaching-learning cycle. They became students of their students" (147).

Inclusion

Brett, another student in my first class, had trouble staying focused, often lost assignments and homework, and struggled with long-term projects. I remember vividly my first conference with Brett's dad (who had forgotten an earlier appointment). He looked around the room, didn't make eye contact, and squirmed in his seat exactly like Brett did each day during morning meeting. I realized I would have to adapt my interactions with Brett *and* his father in order to keep us all on track.

Unfortunately, we didn't know as much as we do now about the challenges of working with students like Brett, who probably had ADD. You may have taught students (whether or not officially diagnosed) with ADD/ADHD, autism, Asperger syndrome, dyslexia, or Tourette syndrome. How much do you know about these learning disabilities? How much do you know about modifying your classroom environment in order to meet the needs of kids who have these conditions? Are there experts in your building or a resource team who could brainstorm ideas with you? How can you help these sometimes worrisome students become welcome members of your classroom?

The Inclusion-Classroom Problem Solver (2007), by Constance McGrath, discusses seven common disabilities: ADD/ADHD, nonverbal learning disabilities, Asperger syndrome and autism, dyslexia, dysgraphia, arithmetical learning disability, and Tourette syndrome. She defines each of these learning challenges; enumerates the concerns of parents, friends, and teachers; and makes specific recommendations for modifying both classroom arrangement and instruction in order to deal with these challenges in a reading/writing workshop.

In *The Kids Behind the Label* (2006), Trudy Knowles writes that modifying instruction is important but reminds us that the social aspect of learning is perhaps even more essential: "Nothing is more important—not test scores, not grades, not a quiet, controlled classroom. Nothing is more important than having a child leave your classroom feeling lifted up and loved. Nothing is more important than challenging, guiding and encouraging the child to go farther than he or she ever thought possible" (128).

Emelie Parker and Tess Pardini, in *"The Words Came Down!"* (2006), describe how fifteen years ago their school used a pull-out model (pulling students out of the regular classroom for small group instruction); scheduling was a huge problem, and ELLs missed the core instruction that took place during reading/writing workshop and math. As the number of ELLs grew, they decided to pull out only those students who were at the preproductive and early productive stages of English acquisition and only for an hour each day. The rest of the time, ESL/ELL teachers worked with those students (and the more proficient ELLs) in their regular classroom.

Intermediate teachers at Singapore American School have been inclusion teachers for the last ten years; they (and their administrators) feel that students' needs are best met by inclusion rather than pull-out instruction. Their classrooms are specifically designed to meet the needs of a range of students. Parents agree that these classrooms, in which the classroom teacher and the support teacher work side by side for the entire two hours of reading/writing/word study every day, have been very successful. Their model has three components:

- Whole-class lessons with some co-teaching for reading and writing
- Differentiated small-group instruction (word study, guided reading) based on specific needs
- Individual conferences

The amount of instructional time for students with learning difficulties immediately increased. They no longer wasted time moving from one classroom to another. They did not miss out on workshop instruction and were therefore able to follow conversations throughout the day that were connected to the workshop. For example, the reading support students were there in the morning when Jodi Bonnette read Marion Dane Bauer's *On My Honor* (1987) and were able to see the connection between the book and their afternoon social studies discussion about how the decisions people make impact others.

Being in the regular classroom all day, ELLs were full participants in the learning community. They no longer had the stigma of being pulled out of the classroom for a portion of the day, which often can hamper their social relationships. This type of inclusion had a dramatic effect on all of the students' learning because they all received extra help since another teacher was in the classroom. The specialist and the classroom teacher, by collaborating on the daily lessons and pooling their resources, were able to meet the needs of all students. When support teachers wrote up an Individualized Educational Support Plan (IESP), they received input on strengths, needs, and goals from the classroom teacher. The classroom and support teachers filled out the child's report card together. The support teacher wrote up an additional narrative about the student's reading/language arts performance and growth.

The upper elementary principal, Marian DeGroot, sees four positive results with the inclusion model:

- Improved learning, because support students have peer models in the classroom; immersion in language and learning with students of all abilities scaffolds their learning
- Maximal time for learning time; no time is lost in transitions from room to room
- Strong collaboration between the classroom teacher and the resource teachers
- Opportunities for students not officially identified as needing extra help to get that support

Classroom teachers and specialists do need to make time to plan their collaborative instruction, which can be difficult, because classroom teachers' schedules are jam-packed. However, meeting just once a week for thirty minutes makes a huge difference. At the Singapore American School, classroom teachers and support teachers are given common times to talk about students or curriculum. Recently a fifth-grade teacher and the ESL/ELL teacher planned two upcoming lessons in just ten minutes. They both felt they had a good grasp of the concepts they would address and how they would divide up the teaching and scaffold the learning-different students in the classroom. This type of ongoing communication is critical to a classroom environment that supports students with learning differences.

It's also important to be careful when considering whether English language or culturally and linguistically different (CLD) learners require resource room support. It's sometimes difficult to distinguish between learning differences and the challenges of learning a new language or dealing with linguistic and cultural differences. Ken Pranksy (2008) writes, "There are so many ways to get a false read with CLD students because the many possible different ways of thinking, feeling, believing, and acting may masquerade as special needs to a teacher unfamiliar with the socio-cultural framework, and because the testing process itself may perpetuate a false read" (88). He suggests we consider the following:

- Referrals of children of color can often be political or otherwise biased.
- We need to be aware of the cultural implications of terms like *special needs* for some families.

▶ It's important to get parents' perspective on their child as a learner and the child's use of their home language.

▶ Academic progress should be viewed in relation to the progress of other members of the classroom community.

▶ There are sometimes biases in the referral process and test materials for CLD students.

▶ We need to examine and reflect on the sociocultural situation in order to find the most supportive learning environment for each student.

In *Teaching Essentials* (2008), Regie Routman writes that when ELLs are misdiagnosed as requiring special education, it's often difficult or even impossible for these children to move back into the regular classroom: "Research shows that when a language minority child is mistakenly placed in special

Book List

Resources for Helping You Implement Differentiation and Inclusion

☐ *The Kids Behind the Label* by Trudy Knowles (2006) (K–12)

☐ *You're Welcome* by Patrick Schwarz and Paula Kluth (2007) (K–12)

☐ *From Disability to Possibility* by Patrick Schwarz (2006) (K–12)

☐ *The Inclusion-Classroom Problem Solver* by Constance McGrath (2007) (K–8)

☐ *A Room with a Differentiated View* by Joanne Yatvin (2004) (K–8)

☐ *Differentiated Learning* by Kathy Paterson (2005) (K–8)

☐ *Differentiation in Action* by Judith Dodge (2006) (4–12)

☐ *Student Diversity* by Faye Brownlie, Catherine Feniak, and Leyton Schnellert) (2006) (K–12)

☐ *The Differentiated School* by Carol Ann Tomlinson, Kay Brimijoin and Lane Navarez (2008) (K–12)

education, it takes an average of six years to reverse this categorization" (8). And that's just to remove the label; the emotional impact may last far longer.

If you want to find out more about inclusion, the three thirty-page booklets that make up *You're Welcome: 30 Innovative Ideas for the Inclusive Classroom*, by Patrick Schwarz and Paula Kluth (2007), and Patrick's heartfelt book *From Disability to Possibility* (2006) contain helpful tips about behavioral support, collaboration and teaming, and differentiating instruction for students with learning differences. As teachers, we need to learn to appreciate and support differences, whether they are the result of cultural diversity,

Ponder Box for Teachers

- How knowledgeable are you about various learning disabilities?

- How well do you differentiate for students with different needs?

- How can you include children with special needs in most or all of your classroom activities?

Ponder Box for Coaches and Principals

- Would the teachers in your school like more information about differentiation and inclusion?

- Do your resource teachers have tips about this topic to share with the rest of the staff?

- Might teachers in your school read some professional books or watch some videos or DVDs about differentiation and inclusion as an interest group, a grade-level focus, or a faculty?

- How can you develop an inclusion program for students with special needs and give classroom teachers and support staff the necessary planning time?

family diversity, or learning diversity. Instead of blaming students or their families when kids struggle, we need to modify, adapt, and think creatively about our materials, teaching methods, and expectations. We need to look past labels and focus on each student's possibilities. As more and more challenging students are placed in your classroom, you'll want to modify the social aspects of your classroom so that *all* students can learn effectively and joyfully as members of a learning community that supports and values differences.

Creating a Community of Learners

Part of building a culturally responsive, inclusive, differentiated classroom hinges on the ability to foster an atmosphere of respect and kindness. Relationships are the axis on which our teaching revolves. All our creative minilessons about comprehension strategies or mentor texts will fall flat if we don't create a safe, loving environment in which students can take risks, share ideas and feelings, and make friends. Lucy Calkins (1994) states, "The quality of writing in our classrooms grows more from the tone, values, and relationships of our classroom communities than from anything else" (142). Somehow, we have to impart our beliefs about justice and compassion to our students so that everyone feels part of the "literacy club."

We've all been in classrooms in which this sense of community and respect are absent. Students talk to each other instead of listening to the teacher during minilessons. Some gaze off into space, and a few wander around the room, getting a drink or sharpening their pencils. When certain students share from the author's chair, you see eye-rolling or hear disparaging comments. These are classrooms in which teachers either don't have the necessary classroom management skills or haven't focused on creating a respectful environment.

What can you do to create a supportive classroom community in which children are engaged, polite, respectful, and caring? The most important thing is to be conscious of your language. Words can destroy a child's confidence or leave scars they remember years later. The language we use also conveys our respect for our students. As the principal at the Manhattan School, Shelley Harwayne (1999) set high standards for talk in her school: "I suggested that teachers imagine that everything they say to their students is somehow broadcast throughout the entire building on a public-address system." She goes on, "There are many city educators and politicians who believe we would transform schools if we put our students in uniforms. I prefer to put my trust in language. We transform schools when we carefully watch how we talk *to* and *about* students, parents, and our colleagues" (22). The Manhattan New School teachers are careful to say that a child is struggling with reading, rather than labeling him as a struggling reader. Rather than saying "my kids" or "my school," they consciously talk about "our school" and "our students." All of Shelley's books have wonderful suggestions for building relationships within classrooms and with the wider community.

In *Life in a Crowded Place* (1992), Ralph Peterson has six suggestions for making your classroom a caring place: ceremonies and rituals, celebrations, conversation, play, routines and jobs, and residency. Conversation is perhaps the most important. "As important as caring talk and discussion are to life and learning in the community, they cannot match the contributions of conversation when it comes to strengthening a community's social fabric" (50). Participating in classroom conversations paves the way for students to become contributors in a democratic society.

Building community is also about getting to know your students. Regie Routman begins *Reading Essentials* (2003) with a chapter about bonding with students. She writes: "Curriculum and standards must first connect with the lives and spirits of our children if we're to have any lasting success. Unless we reach into our students' hearts, we have no entry into their minds" (12). She goes on to explain how the personal connections do more than provide insights into book choices or writing topics; they are the heart of responsive teaching.

Kitty Strauss is a fourth-grade teacher in Colorado who has created a supportive classroom for all her students. On the first day of school, she begins by sharing bits from her life so that her students know her as a person. In turn, she works hard to get to know as much as she can about each student's family, friends, and interests. During the first few weeks of school, Kitty spends a great deal of time sharing books and talking about how she and her students can support and encourage one another. She knows that students won't reveal their feelings in their poetry, share their opinions about a book, or try a new form of writing if she hasn't set a tone of respect and shown students they can take risks without fear of ridicule or criticism. The books she chooses to read depend on the composition of each class and what these students seem to need most in terms of trust, safety, respect, and self-direction. Kitty and her students talk a lot about what they all need to be the best possible learners in their classroom, and she explains her role in ensuring they are safe, respected, and challenged to grow. They discuss the importance of creating a peaceful and vibrant literacy community in which that can happen, how to support one another, how to conquer fears, and how to respond to bullying. Here are some books Kitty has used to build a sense of community within her classroom:

- *Peace Begins with You* by Katharine Scholes (1994) (peaceful environments for learning)
- *High as a Hawk* by T. A. Barron (2004) (persevering through struggles)

▶ *Owen and Mzee: The True Story of a Remarkable Friendship* by Isabella Hatkoff, Craig Hatkoff, and Paula Kahumbu (2006) (the need to support one another)

▶ *Thank You, Mr. Falker* by Patricia Polacco (2001) (struggles with learning)

▶ *Thunder Cake* by Patricia Polacco (1997) (conquering your fears)

▶ *The Recess Queen* by Alexia O'Neill (2002) (bullying)

▶ *Hooway for Wodney Wat* by Helen Lester (1999) (teasing)

▶ *My Secret Bully* by Trudy Ludwig (2005) (bullying)

▶ *Stand Tall, Molly Lou Melon* by Patty Lovell (2001) (bullying)

▶ *Mr. Lincoln's Way* by Patricia Polacco (2001) (bullying)

▶ *The Bully Blockers Club* by Teresa Bateman (2006) (bullying)

Each time I walk into Kitty's classroom, I am astonished by its tone—each student is respectful of every other in every way. During writing workshop, I marvel at how attentively her students listen to her lessons and how thoughtfully they interject with constructive comments that reveal the depth of their learning. Students read their pieces of writing in a conference with Kitty, with a partner, in small groups, or for the entire class from the author's chair. As I listened in on a peer conference the last time I visited, a student said, "I know you worked very hard on your overall structure to help it be more understandable to the reader. I can see how you revised by moving some sentences around and adding in some other sentences. I encourage you to continue doing that as a writer. You might also think about adding in some more detail with striking verbs like Mrs. Strauss showed us yesterday. Let's see if you can find one right now that you can work on." Comments like this are proof that Kitty has instilled a deep respect in her students as they relate to one another. This sort of considerate, deep listening takes place because Kitty believes in creating a classroom that will support learning for all her students.

Regie Routman (2008) writes, "Celebration is about finding the joy in teaching and learning and seeing the child's accomplishments, no matter how small" (31). Celebration is showing that we care about each student; it is at the heart of effective teaching. One way to set a positive tone is by celebrating each student, as Eliza Lewis does on individual "compliment charts." The compliments poster is a collaborative exercise that requires teams of four or five students to brainstorm positive ideas about a classmate and negotiate which statements to include so that the class creates an accurate and well-rounded "snapshot" of each child. The child being discussed is present and participates in all the steps of the process thus receiving heaps of affirmation.

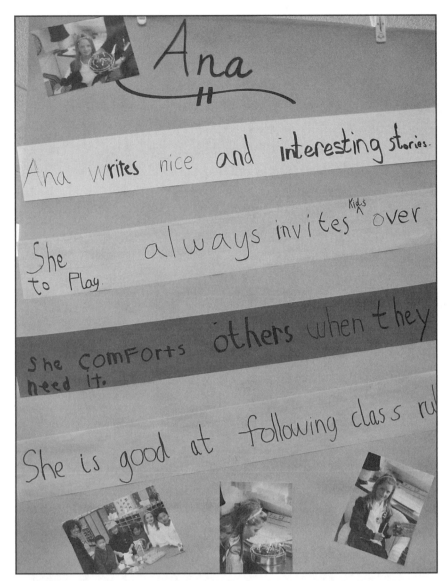

A Compliment Chart from Eliza Lewis' Classroom

Carol Dulac's Class Greetings

Many parents have reported that the poster is a source of pride and hangs on the child's bedroom wall the rest of the year. One parent shared that she had to stop her daughter from sleeping with her poster! Ana is a wonderful child and student and probably totally unaware of how much she was appreciated and valued by her classmates. The activity and poster gave her an opportunity to see herself through other people's eyes.

Other teachers do similar activities for birthdays or as part of student portfolios. You can also teach ways to interact positively, disagree politely, and practice listening and speaking skills during class meetings. Carol Dulac has her third graders practice how to greet one another politely. Every morning students gather in a circle and choose from a variety of greeting activities:

▶ The handshake

▶ Skip one (or two, three, four, and so on)

▶ Last names (students choose a name from a stack of cards—Miss Campbell, Mr. Smith, and so on—and greet on another as that person)

▶ Greetings in another language

▶ The backward ball (adapted from an idea in the *Responsive Classroom* newsletter). Each Friday students greet one another by throwing a ball from person to person, the student throwing the ball saying the name of the student to whom the ball is thrown. When everyone has been greeted, the students throw the ball in reverse order. (They time the activity each week to see if they can beat their record.)

Activities like these ensure that each student is recognized individually and develops a sense of being part of a community of learners in which everyone is respected.

Karen Casto and Jennifer Audley, in their book *In Our School* (2008), write about actively building a positive sense of community both within and outside their school. They create routines and structures for working together in classrooms, develop schoolwide events, and bring parents into teaching and learning as partners. They foster a sense of community through morning circles and welcoming daily routines. Karen and Jennifer also describe yearly events, such as sixth-grade promotion and family nights, that help build a sense of community within a school. Here are just a few of the many ways to improve the social environment in your classroom in order to create a sense of community:

▶ Be conscious of the language you use with students and families.

▶ Share stories about your own life.

▶ Get to know your students' interests.

▶ Teach students to be polite to one another, to teachers, and to visitors.

▶ Hold class meetings about problems and appropriate ways to respond to one another.

▶ Brainstorm lists of supportive language and behavior.

▶ Use events and rituals to create a sense of community.

▶ Hold frequent celebrations (of kindness, strengths, and accomplishments).

▶ Use books and writing to bond and connect.

▶ Share literature about cooperation, justice, respect, and friendship.

▶ Laugh and sing together!

▶ Set high expectations for respectful behavior.

▶ Nurture a sense of belonging.

▶ Ensure that parents feel welcome in your classroom.

Teaching and learning are always about the relationships that are nurtured within a community of learners. This is the heart of Ralph Peterson's message in *Life in a Crowded Place* (1992). The rituals and routines we set up and the language we use help *all* our students feel like welcome members of a joyful learning community.

Book List

Resources for Creating a Community of Learners

☐ *In Our School* by Karen Casto and Jennifer Audley (2008) (K–5)

☐ *Life in a Crowded Place* by Ralph Peterson (1992) (K–5)

☐ *Teaching Essentials* by Regie Routman (2008) (K–8)

☐ *Going Public* by Shelley Harwayne (1999) (K–5)

☐ *Lifetime Guarantees* by Shelley Harwayne (2000) (K–5)

58

Ponder Box for Teachers

- Where would you place yourself on the Community row of the rubric that follows?

- How do you celebrate learning in your classroom?

- How do you foster respectful behavior in your classroom?

- How do you address problems that arise in the classroom?

- How can you further support a positive learning community in your classroom?

Ponder Box for Coaches and Principals

- Where would you place your school on the Community row of the rubric that follows?

- How do you foster respectful behavior at your school?

- How can you further support a positive learning community in your school?

Classroom Environment and Community of Learners (Teacher Rubric)

NOVICE	APPRENTICE	PRACTITIONER	LEADER
		Community	
☐ There is little modification of classroom work for needs of different learners; my program for ELLs and learners with special needs is primarily "pull-out" and/or limited; students tend to work in isolation or in a competitive way	☐ There are minimal modifications for ELLs and learners with special needs (e.g., I tell them to read books two or more times); my program for ELLs and learners with special needs is primarily "pull-out" but includes some "push-in" and inclusion; I have some rapport with my students; there is a general sense of community; I introduce some cooperative learning activities	☐ Some of my instruction is differentiated and modified for ELLs and learners with special needs based on systemic school-wide practices (e.g., I use visual cues when reading aloud); my program for ELLs and other learners with special needs is a combination of inclusion, "push-in," and "pull-out"; ESL/ELL and resource teachers sometimes work in my classroom; students support and encourage one another and sometimes collaborate; I focus on building a sense of community	☐ My teaching and materials are culturally responsive and inclusive; I differentiate and modify my instruction for ELLs and learners with special needs; ELLs and learners with special needs have mostly an inclusion and "push-in" program, but there is a "pull-out" program as needed for some students; my back-and-forth communication with the ESL/ELL teachers and resource staff is clear and cooperative; I encourage a risk-taking and collaborative environment in which students support and encourage one another in a respectful, thoughtful, literate community of learners

Classroom Environment and Community of Learners (School Rubric)

NOVICE	APPRENTICE	PRACTITIONER	LEADER
		Community	
☐ In most classrooms, there is little modification of classroom work for needs of different learners; programs for ELLs and learners with special needs are primarily "pull-out" and/or limited; in most classrooms students tend to work in isolation or in a competitive way	☐ Teachers make a few modifications for ELLs and learners with special needs (e.g., students are told to read books two or more times); programs for ELLs and learners with special needs are primarily "pull-out"; in a few classrooms, there is some "push-in" and inclusion; most teachers have some rapport with their students; in most classrooms, there is a general sense of community; most teachers introduce some cooperative learning activities	☐ In most classrooms, teachers differentiate and modify some instruction for ELLs and learners with special needs based on systemic schoolwide practices (e.g., teachers use visual cues when reading aloud); in most classrooms, programs for ELLs and learners with special needs are a combination of inclusion, "push-in," and "pull-out"; ESL/ELL and resource teachers work in most classrooms; in most classrooms, students support and encourage one another and sometimes collaborate; most teachers focus on building a sense of community	☐ In all classrooms, learning and materials are culturally responsive and inclusive; teachers in all classrooms differentiate and modify their instruction for ELLs and learners with special needs; ELLs and learners with special needs have mostly inclusion and "push-in" programs, but there are some "pull-out" programs as needed for some students; back-and-forth communication with the ESL/ELL teachers and resource staff is clear and cooperative; teachers in all classrooms encourage a risk-taking and collaborative environment in which students support and encourage one another in respectful, thoughtful, literate communities of learners

Getting to the Essence of Learning and Teaching

For many years, schools and teachers emphasized *teaching*. Educators used curriculum to decide *what to teach*, they used pedagogy to decide *how to teach*, and they used the calendar to decide *when to teach* as well as *when they had taught*. But research has helped us to make the shift from the *teaching* to the *learning* that occurs in our classrooms. In *Learning by Doing: A Handbook for Professional Learning Communities at Work* (2006), Richard DuFour and his colleagues demonstrate how to emphasize *learning*. Instead of asking, "What will I teach? When will I teach it?" we should be asking, "What do we want students to learn? How will we know when each student has learned it?"

This means we have to shift our position as members of *teaching* communities and become fully engaged members of *learning* communities. As Carrie and I read more about this shift toward a student-centered focus, we decided that rather than using the phrase *teaching and learning*, we would place *learning* first, both in the rubric and in the title of this chapter.

Now that we've set the stage, on with the show.

I once scanned all the illustrations in the classic book *Caps for Sale* (1968) by Esphyr Slobodkina and projected them, one by one, during a presentation I gave on the many hats teachers wear. A teacher is many things in a classroom—an observer, a mentor, a coach, a counselor, a moderator, a learner, a researcher, and sometimes even a nurse! This chapter explores five ways to maintain a nurturing environment for learning and teaching while balancing all those roles:

❶ Creating student-centered classrooms.

❷ Promoting more student talk.

❸ Demonstrating, guiding, and conferring.

❹ Facilitating student learning.

❺ Teaching effectively through classroom management.

The first two have to do with *learning* and students' role in the classroom. The next three are about *teaching* and the teacher's role.

Creating Student-Centered Classrooms

In addition to changing their classroom's physical and social environment, teachers can move toward more child-centered and responsive teaching by shifting the ways they interact with students. Where does your classroom fall on a continuum between teacher-centered and student-centered? What does a student-centered classroom look like?

Over the past twenty years, professional books and articles have recommended that we build *student-centered classrooms*. When the term first caught hold in the 1980s, a number of teachers assumed it meant the classroom now was led by the students; the teacher stood back and watched and listened, then allowed the children to direct all their own learning. Fortunately, that was not what the researchers had in mind. The term conveys an expectation that teaching is guided by a curriculum and a set of goals for students to achieve; however, instead of following a rigid sequence of lessons, teachers choose the route to this destination by observing their particular students' unique strengths and needs and then ask questions and introduce activities that help them along the way. Teachers still drive the bus and serve as tour guides, because they have the most experience and expertise.

It's important for you to know your curriculum and standards, as well as the developmental stages of literacy acquisition. It's also important to know your students. Learning the names of your students and something about them right away is one of the first ways you can create student-centered classrooms and schools. Following Shelley Harwayne through the halls of the Manhattan New School, I was amazed when she greeted every student we passed by name, often asking about a child's sibling or upcoming birthday party. This strategy was intentional. In *Going Public* (1999), she explains that she delights in knowing the names of all her students and their families. She views being a "knower of names" as part of her job description. While she was a superintendent in New York, Shelley applied these same principles to her work with principals and teachers around the city. Learning names is an important first step in creating a school in which each student and teacher feels valued.

Many years ago, as a classroom teacher, Donald Graves memorized the names of all his students before school even began. As he matched names to faces on the first day, he began collecting words to match each student's strengths and interests. In many workshops, I try this activity, borrowed from Don; it can be very powerful. Take a piece of paper and divide it into three columns. In the first column, write down all your students' names. Which ones come to mind first? Which student do you think of last? Do you remember boys or girls more easily? In the second column, list two or three interests, favorite books, or characteristics for each student. Again, which ones are easy? Which students don't you know as well? The third column is for more specific information about each student and may remain blank until you get to know each student better.

In *A Sea of Faces* (2006), Don Graves talks about working in a classroom and shares poems he wrote about the teacher and her students. (The poems will remind you of many students you've taught.) Could you write a poem about each of your students? Here is part of his poem "We Have All Come from Somewhere" (100):

> I call all my children
> By their first name
> By the end of the first day.
> Then I begin to write down
> What is special about each one.
> I carry their names in my head
> And as I go through the list
> I think of some good thing,
> Some one thing, that each child knows
> That is unique or wonderful.

In a student-centered classroom, instruction is shaped and guided by the teacher's interactions with students. Responsive teaching is integral. Carrie experienced a dramatic shift in her pedagogy when she first learned about student-centered teaching." I'll let Carrie tell her own story:

> Luckily, I was able to observe a master teacher and writer, Mary Ellen Giacobbe, who was consulting in our school district. As I watched her in a writing workshop, I noticed how she began each day with a focused minilesson, but then she did something that challenged my former paradigm of teaching. After her lesson, Mary Ellen began to move around the room, talking to individual children about their writing. As I listened to these writing conferences, I realized that she was saying something unique to each student based on their responses to her questions. Once I started doing this with my own students I saw immediate results—they had much more ownership of their learning. This doesn't sound so radical now, but this method of conferring was a new concept to me in 1984.

Promoting Student Talk

Student-centered classrooms hum with conversations. Students contribute ideas during shared and guided writing and reading activities. They share their writing and reading responses with partners, in small groups, and during individual conferences. Conversations support the thinking about the texts that students read and write. Talk is the medium on which learning floats.

Recently, Carrie had the privilege of introducing the concept of talking as a way to support reading comprehension to a class of fifth graders. Several other teachers were observing the lesson. Carrie began reading aloud *The Cello of Mr. O* (2004), by Jane Cutler and Greg Couch, articulating her thinking about what she read as well. After a few pages, she asked the kids to turn and talk with their partners about a specific prompt. The observing teachers were amazed at the sophisticated conversations the students had. One small tweak—making a read-aloud interactive—had generated open-ended partner conversation and impacted the students' thinking and learning. After three days of this type of instruction, the students in this classroom pleaded with their teacher to continue partner talk, telling her, "It helps us understand the stories better."

Debriefing with the teachers later, Carrie talked about ways that they could support this type of student talk by listening in on the discussions and interjecting teaching points when appropriate. She showed the group how she recorded her insights on sticky notes in order to guide future minilessons. Students were in charge of the conversations; teachers became facilitators and side-by-side learning guides.

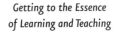

Literacy Coach Jodi Bonnette Listens as Students Turn and Talk to Each Other

Later, while the students were reading independently, Carrie conducted a guided lesson with a group of students whom their teacher felt needed more support in talking through their ideas. Carrie read aloud the first few pages of *Canada Geese Quilt* by Natalie Kinesey-Warnock (1992). Then she asked the group to read the next few pages silently and, taking a cue from *Comprehension Through Conversation* by Maria Nichols (2006), gave them a specific prompt: "This girl lives in a very different setting than you do. How is Ariel's classroom different from yours?" (Students who are just beginning to share their thinking need more scaffolding than the open-ended prompt, "What are you thinking right now?")

As the group read quietly, Carrie asked two of the students what they were thinking and took notes to help her guide the subsequent group discussion. Later, as the kids talked, it took a few minutes for them to realize that instead of asking questions, Carrie was there to facilitate *their* discussion. Once they did, they began animatedly tossing ideas back and forth, piggybacking off one another's thinking. Their teacher marveled at the natural and sophisticated level of talk she heard, saying, "I've never heard you talk so much about your reading and share so many of your thoughts. I can hardly wait to hear what you think tomorrow as you read on in the book." This teacher and her colleagues, as well as the students, saw how important it is to promote more student talk through open-ended questions.

Increasing the amount of student talk enhances both engagement and comprehension. Maria Nichols (2006) challenges each of us to create conversational classrooms in which children use language to negotiate and construct meaning. We can embed this conversation in our literacy instruction by conducting interactive read-alouds, by asking students to turn and talk, and by having them talk about their independent reading with a partner. Rather than leading conversations, we can ask more open-ended questions and facilitate student talk during guided reading, small-group lessons, and sharing from the author's chair. We can also support authentic conversations during reading and writing conferences. The benefit of this sort of purposeful talk extends beyond the classroom; these reflective, articulate, respectful speakers will more easily become full, creative participants in a democratic society.

Demonstrating, Guiding, and Conferring

As Carrie read and discussed *The Cello of Mr. O* with the class and then discussed *Canada Geese Quilt* with the small group, she supported learning in three specific ways. She began by *demonstrating* her own comprehension strategies; she then provided time for guided *practice*; and she ended by *celebrating* the impressive "thinking work" the students were doing. Her instruction is a pedagogical doorway between two complementary theories of education: conditions for learning and the gradual release of responsibility.

Conditions for Learning

Brian Cambourne (1988) outlines seven conditions of learning that he uncovered in his research about how children acquire language:

- demonstration
- immersion
- practice
- approximations
- feedback/support/celebrations
- responsibility
- expectations

These conditions are the foundation of a responsive philosophy of teaching and learning and apply to everything we learn, whether we're children or adults. What does this look like in a classroom?

Anne Klein is working with her fifth graders on crafting strong leads for their vignettes. She starts by *demonstrating*, writing about when she got lost in a cave in college. She drafts several leads using her document camera, the class discusses which ones are most effective, and Anne combines parts of several attempts into one strong lead. She next *immerses* the students in discovering the characteristics of strong leads as together they scour novels and picture books for great leads that pull readers in, then list the different techniques that authors use. Students each share one lead they find and tell the class why it is effective. They discover that authors use questions, description, and dialogue as "hooks" to invite readers into the story. Anne writes these techniques, along with one or two examples, on a chart for future reference and makes a handout about leads for students to put in their writing workshop notebooks.

Next, Anne has students *practice* crafting leads in their own writing, asking them to select a story they are working on and experiment with— *approximate*—a variety of leads. Then they read their leads to a partner and discuss which one works best, giving and receiving immediate *feedback*. The session ends with students "popping up" to explain their changes. Finally, Anne offers *feedback* and *support* in individual conferences and *celebrates* as students share their strong leads from the author's chair.

The *responsibility* for incorporating the strategy then shifts to the students, as they tuck this idea of grabbing leads into their toolbox of writing strategies. Anne now *expects* her students to think intentionally about their leads in future writing. She writes, "This process closely follows Brian Cambourne's conditions for learning—students need the time to use and make approximations with feedback in order to become more fluid with trying and using a variety of leads in their writing." Anne finds these conditions for learning so powerful that they are posted on the wall by her desk as a reminder when she plans instruction.

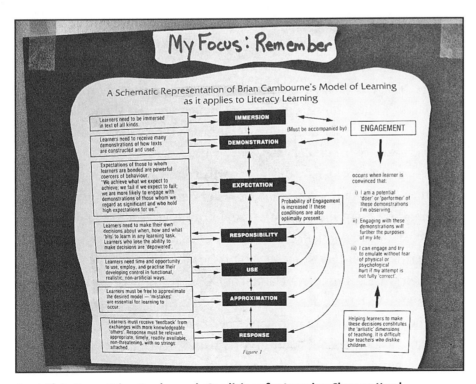

Anne Klein Keeps Brian Cambourne's Conditions for Learning Close at Hand

Gradual Release

Brian Cambourne's conditions for learning are the foundation on which the gradual release model of learning is constructed, which in turn provides the framework and structure for a reading/writing workshop as described by Lucy Calkins, Regie Routman, Irene Fountas, Gay Su Pinnell, and others. The gradual release model includes demonstration, shared demonstrations, guided practice, and independent practice. During the demonstration phase, the teacher does most of the work as he shares his writing or thinks aloud about his reading strategies. During the shared demonstration phase, students chime in with suggestions and questions. Guided practice occurs in small guided reading groups, in writing groups, or during individual conferences in which students do most of the work, but the teacher is there to guide and support them. Students then need lots of opportunities to practice the new skill independently in their own reading and writing. The goal is to remove a bit of scaffolding, bit by bit, based on each student's needs, so that eventually they can demonstrate the strategy independently and transfer that knowledge to new contexts.

Here's another classroom example. Kitty Strauss, a fourth-grade teacher in Denver, Colorado, designates sixty minutes each day for writing workshop. Based on some gaps in her students' writing, she decides to focus on elevating the "inner story" of a narrative through interior dialogue, or "thought-shots" (Lane 1993, 44). Kitty *demonstrates* this technique using her own writing, describing what her character is thinking and feeling; next, she and her students draft a short piece (*shared writing*) that incorporates what the protagonist is thinking.

Student pairs then share any thoughtshots they have added to their own writing, along with reflections about the effectiveness of the strategy. For instance, Eli tells Melissa that her thoughtshots helped him understand her feelings in her story about a dance competition. He thinks it would be even more helpful if she adds more specifics about how her nervousness was displayed—sweaty hands, cold feet, wobbly legs.

Kitty notices that a few students are struggling with this concept, so she pulls these students together and provides *guided practice* using mentor texts, showing them more examples and providing additional support. She also provides *guided practice* during individual writing conferences. At the end of writing workshop, students discuss how they incorporated this idea to make their writing stronger. Melissa shares her line: "I just kept thinking how nervous I was to be solo dancing in front of that enormous audience. I found myself being slightly dizzy with nerves before I went on stage."

After this minilesson, many of Kitty's students begin to write *independently* with more specificity as they try to capture the details of moments in time. At the end of the writing workshop, Kitty collects a few of the students' writing folders in order to evaluate the effect of her minilesson on their writing. The concept of gradual release is the framework on which she builds her teaching.

Both Anne and Kitty provide just the right amount of support based on what they know about their students. They first demonstrate, then provide guidance through additional shared reading/writing activities as students practice the new skill. They offer additional support during individual conferences. As you plan your units of study, have you provided each of these components? Regie Routman (2008, 91) claims that too often we leap from demonstration into practice without enough "hand holding" and shared demonstration.

Facilitating Student Learning

Besides demonstrating, guiding, and conferring, how else can you facilitate learning? Many teachers understand the goals for student learning and are able to design units and map out a plan of how to get there. However, the true *art* of teaching is the ability to design student-centered activities and structures so that students engage in higher-level talk and learning. Experienced teachers have honed the craft of asking thought-provoking, open-ended questions that launch high-level discussions. Questions with "right answers" are easy; the biggest teaching challenge is posing questions that cause students to ponder, think, problem solve, and share their thinking with one another. After thinking aloud with your own reading or writing, pose questions that begin with *How . . . ?, Why . . . ?,* or *What do you think about . . . ?* As your students talk and problem solve, circulate and take notes to use in your next minilesson to propel your students even further in their learning.

There is also an art to interjecting small comments that move a conversation forward or bridge one observation to another. When Carrie was demonstrating the art of facilitating conversations, one teacher commented: "It's so different from other teachers, who seem to *pull* the students along. You're gently nudging from the *side* and from the *rear.* You let the students take the lead and just guide them when needed."

Roaming through a first-grade classroom, I beam when I overhear a discussion between partners who are sharing the how-to books they have written: "I like how you put in the part about kicking the soccer ball off your toe, but I think you forgot the step about pointing it at another player." Down the hall, I squat down and listen in as a cluster of fifth graders discuss the questions raised in Jon Muth's book, *The Three Questions* (2002). One student says, "I think that he's right that 'the only important time is now.'" Another student responds, "But isn't looking at the past important to help us to know what to do now? And if we don't think about the future, then how will we act today to make sure to impact the future in a positive way?" During these discussions the teachers are taking anecdotal notes and listening in to learn more about the thinking going on and possible next steps for these students. Once in a while, they interject with a question to keep the flow going or engage a quiet student.

Further down the corridor a fourth-grade classroom offers a very different picture of "learning." Students listen silently while their teacher gives thirty minutes of instructions for a major writing project. This isn't learning; it's an exercise in listening and remembering. There are no conditions for learning, no gradual release. The way language is being used is also quite different, as is the degree of student engagement.

The language that teachers use in the classroom sets the tone for learning. *The Power of Our Words* (2007), by Paula Denton, begins, "Language is one of the most powerful tools available to teachers." She offers much-needed insight into why and how we must choose our language thoughtfully to help students construct understanding, develop respectful and connected relationships, and monitor their learning. Paula discusses how to use language to help children envision success; to pose open-ended questions that stretch children's thinking; and to listen and offer meaningful, specific encouragement to children. We can guide student learning most effectively when our language is action oriented, brief, and authentic. And perhaps most difficult of all, we need to learn when to be silent and when to listen.

Peter Johnston, in *Choice Words: How Our Language Affects Children's Learning* (2004), also demonstrates how the language that teachers use dramatically impacts the evolution of their students' thinking and therefore their success in school and in life. Kitty Strauss wrote Carrie about how much *Choice Words* impacted her teaching:

Choice Words stresses the importance of intentional teacher language. So this year, about thirty intermediate teachers in our district have been using intentional teacher language, practicing diagnostic guided reading instruction, and having reflective conversations about how our students have grown because of our purposeful planning and language.

Intentional teacher language has changed our students from often appearing dependent, helpless, and disengaged to demonstrating rigor, stamina, independence, and pride in their work. We first created a safe, nurturing environment where everyone felt important and valued. Then we began naming and noticing strategies that lead to successful outcomes. We "named/defined/noticed" what rigor, independence, stamina, and quality work (RISQ) looked like and sounded like in our classrooms. We named and celebrated "struggle," shared strategies for "powering through challenges," offered suggestions about ways to move when you're stuck, and reflected together about how it feels when you succeed because of hard work. We shared our struggles daily, along with tips about how to "power through" them.

At the end of each day I asked, "Who struggled through something hard today? How did you get through it? When/where might you use that same strategy outside of our classroom?" I took myself out of the "power" role by simply changing the way I asked questions: when they'd say, "I don't get it," I'd ask, "What part *do* you understand?" and "What are you thinking you might try in order to move through the hard part?"

My words have clearly empowered students. It's the result of a simple "tweaking" and "finessing" of the way I approach our conversations. *They* can name and notice, strategize, make choices, struggle, take a breath, power through, and own it. They know what rigor, independence, stamina, and quality work look like and feel like. I just ask, "How did you do that?" and "How did that make you feel?" Choosing just the right words has helped foster their belief that they can behave in strategic ways to solve most problems that arise. As teachers, we can help our students understand that true learning involves "struggle," that it's a natural process to be celebrated. With the right words, we can truly create magic in our classrooms.

Choice Words helped us examine our beliefs and values around the important role the teacher has in shaping the learning community within a classroom. The book highlights how very important teacher modeling and teacher language are in that process. At IRA this year, Peter said that classrooms/teachers have two big stressors working against them in the pursuit of deep conversations, inquiry-based learning, and empowered critical thinkers—shortage of time and a high-decibel noise level! Both are real constraints that can counteract what the research in *Choice Words* has found to be most effective in developing students with strong agency around who they are as learners. He said that stressors tend to make people want closure, not open-ended ongoing learning/conversation. As we try to intentionally use the language that we know will change how a child views himself or a class views itself, we struggle to keep it authentic, keep it deep, and keep it consistent—time constraints or not!

The books by Peter Johnston and Paula Denton have made a huge impression on many teachers. Both authors suggest that the ways in which we talk to children has a significant impact on the tone of the classroom.

The language that we use helps establish relationships and a sense of community and helps shape how students view themselves. We need to remember that children deserve the same respect we offer our family and very best friends if they are to feel comfortable and confident enough to move forward in their learning.

Book List

Resources for Helping You Improve Learning and Teaching in Your Classroom

- ☐ *Going Public* by Shelley Harwayne (Chapter 2) (1999) (K–5)
- ☐ *Comprehension Through Conversation* by Maria Nichols (2006) (K–5)
- ☐ *The Whole Story* by Brian Cambourne (1988) (K–5)
- ☐ *The Power of Our Words* by Paula Denton (2007) (K–8)
- ☐ *Choice Words* by Peter Johnston (2004) (K–8)
- ☐ *Positive Teacher Talk for Better Classroom Management* by Deborah Diffily and Charlotte Sassman (2006) (K–2)

Ponder Box for Teachers

- Which conditions of learning are strongly in place in your classroom and which ones do you want to learn more about?

- Which elements of gradual release instruction are in place in your classroom and which need to be stronger?

- What is the ratio of student talk to teacher talk in your classroom? In what parts of your instructional day might you increase student talk?

Ponder Box for Coaches and Principals

- Which conditions of learning are strongly in place in classrooms in your school and which ones should you focus on in professional development with teachers?

- Which elements of gradual release instruction are in place in your school classrooms? Which elements do teachers need more support in understanding?

- As you visit classrooms, is there a strong proportion of productive student talk versus teacher talk? If not, what type of professional development or reading would help teachers better understand the critical need for more student talk?

Teaching Effectively Through Classroom Management

Creating a student-centered classroom, promoting student talk, thinking carefully about the language you use, employing gradual release and scaffolding, offering choice, providing time for practice, building stamina—none of those qualities will be effective if you haven't mastered the basics of classroom management. Students appreciate choice and flexibility, but they also need predictability and structure. Your classroom should have the same hum and buzz and productivity as any other working environment.

Good teachers make teaching look easy. A teacher like Anne Klein runs a tight ship, but her students learn a tremendous amount in the year they're with her. She has a predictable routine and schedule. I know that any morning I visit her classroom there will be writing workshop before recess and reading workshop after recess. Anne provides lots of opportunities for talk, but there are also times when the room is quiet so students can sink into their writing or get lost in the book they're reading. Before each transition, students push in their chairs and clear off their desks, so the room has a sense of order. Anne has had some really challenging students over the years, but I can rarely spot them when I visit. James Stronge (2007) found that one of the main talents of effective teachers is the ability to prevent negative behavior by proactively setting clear rules and routines for the students, as well as establishing trust and rapport. Experienced teachers follow up by helping students monitor their own behavior within the expectations set and develop appropriate consequences. Anne does all these things so calmly that her room exudes a sense of order and calm.

Three essential aspects of classroom management are:

▶ routines, schedules, and rituals

▶ planning and organization

▶ discipline

Routines, Schedules and Rituals

All children need a predictable schedule and clear expectations. For some students, your classroom may be a haven of calm compared with their lives at home. This doesn't mean that school is boring. The content, your mini-lessons, the books you share, and the specific units all provide variety. The predictability comes with the structure of reading/writing workshop, your daily routines, and the rituals you set up. Karen Casto and Jennifer Audley (2008) comment: "In school, routines help create a familiar, safe environment so that children and adults can focus their energies on learning" (41).

Janet Angelillo (2008) lists a clear and detailed summary of classroom organization and management. She describes how to support teaching through:

▶ transitions

▶ materials

▶ making sure students know what to bring to learning

▶ lateness policies

▶ bathroom and water breaks

▶ announcements and attendance

▶ work rules

▶ finishing work

▶ watching the time

An important aspect of classroom management is the way you start each day. Primary teacher Debbie Miller felt that the morning sharing in her primary classroom wasn't always productive; she also wanted to bridge what students were learning at school with their lives at home. She decided to begin each morning by calling out each student's name, preceded by a warm, "Good morning." Students respond by sharing snippets of the reading and writing they have done at home. On her DVD *Literary Attendance* (2006), a boy describes how he is teaching his little brother how to read, a girl talks about how that morning she wrote down her dream so she wouldn't forget it, and another girl shares a book she's brought from home. With this ten-minute ritual, Debbie connects with each child and discovers how her students are applying what they learn in school to their lives outside the classroom. If too many students have stories to tell on a given day, have them turn and talk to

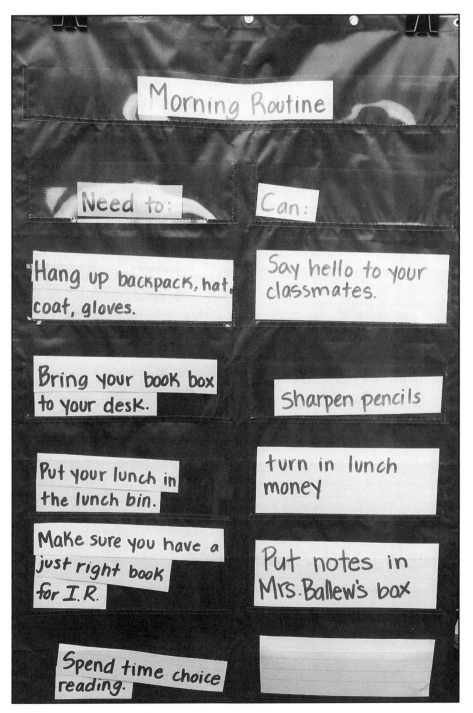

Sherri Ballew's Morning Routines

their neighbors. You may also want to keep a clipboard with anecdotal notes handy so you can briefly keep track of who has shared and what they said.

The students in Megan Sloan's classroom tend to trickle in at different times because of bus schedules and traffic; students know they are expected to hang up their coat, sign in, and then find a book to read with a partner. Their day begins with the peaceful ritual of reading authentically and sharing books with their friends. Megan also launches every reading and writing workshop with a minilesson, her students snuggled up next to her on the rug. They know this will be followed by time to read and write independently, and many students come to school thinking about the book they're reading or what they plan to write that day. Each day Megan confers with several readers and writers and meets with small groups for literature circles or guided reading. Her students know that she will read a chapter from a book every day after lunch and that the day always ends with a hug or a "high five" as they head home. This predictability gives a sense of order and comfort.

Since many of Sherri Ballew's students are English language learners (ELLs), she is careful to provide directions both orally and in writing. She uses a pocket chart to remind students what they're supposed to do when they enter the classroom each day. The classroom is soon filled with the quiet sound of pages turning as everyone reads a just-right book. This routine fosters independence in all her students and supports ELLs.

Of course, these routines don't just fall into place automatically. Each part of the schedule, even simple tasks such as coming to the rug quietly, requires explicit teaching and practice.

Once you have the structures in place, how do you make the transition from one activity to another so that your students don't lose valuable time for learning? Megan uses music or verbal signals ("eyes on me") to signal transitions rather than raising her voice or clapping; other teachers call out a specific phrase or use a chime. The staff at the Manhattan New School created a list of ideas for signaling transitions that can be found in *Going Public* (Harwayne 1999, 122, 123). You may want to brainstorm ideas with your colleagues, then compare your ideas with this list.

Planning and Organization

Another trait of effective teachers is the ability to be consistent and anticipate problems. Several years ago, Carrie volunteered to teach in a windowless first-grade classroom, and it occurred to her that she should be prepared in case the lights ever went out—the six-year-olds would probably panic. She purchased a couple of flashlights and put them in opposite corners of the room. Her first announcement on the first day of school was that if the lights ever went out, students were to get in a line, hold hands, and crawl on the

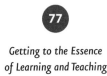

floor behind her so no one would get hurt bumping into furniture. Sure enough, the lights did go out, about thirty minutes before the end of the day! Unfortunately, neither flashlight was close to where she was at that moment; however, her planning paid off. The scared young learners got on the floor, grabbed hands with someone else, and became part of the "train" moving across the room. After what seemed forever, they all made it out into the hallway bright with sunshine streaming in from a skylight. If Carrie hadn't anticipated this glitch, that first day could have been traumatic.

I'm known for my mania for organization: my family laughs at my copious sticky notes and lists. (When the kids were younger, before I left on a trip, I used to leave "lesson plans" for my husband—a white notebook with carpool and sports schedules, homework deadlines, dates of dentist appointments, and reminders to water the plants!) I'm teased about the checklist I print out every time I pack for a trip—but I always find one or two things I would have otherwise forgotten.

It takes me between seventy-five and a hundred emails to set up a visit to one international school. In addition to the topics and focus, we email back and forth about dates, visas, flights, where I'll stay, how many days I'll be able to work with teachers, what equipment the school has, and times for workshops. I ask my contact to send me school standards, literacy documents, and sample report cards, as well as the names of all the teachers and the titles of the books they've read in professional book study groups. By the time I arrive, I know a lot about the school; the materials I need are ready, the room is already set up with comfortable tables, and I can focus on getting to know teachers and delving into literacy and assessment. I find that the more I plan in advance, the more I don't have to worry about details and logistics and can concentrate on *teaching*.

The same is true in your classroom. There's simply too much you hope to accomplish during the school year. If you have all the materials and books you need and you've mapped out your units of study and created a predictable schedule for reading/writing workshop, you can focus on *teaching*. Regie Routman writes in *Teaching Essentials* (2008), "One of the best ways to keep students engaged (in which case, classroom management becomes a non-issue) is to teach with a sense of urgency—that is with the expectation that there is not a minute to lose, that every moment must be used for purposeful instruction, assessment, practice, coaching, and so on" (96).

Teachers have to be organized. This means that before she gathers her class together on the rug, Megan Sloan has planned her minilesson within her unit of study based on recent assessments of her students' writing. She has decided what her explicit teaching will be and even thought through some possible student responses to the lesson and how she can address them. She has Jane Yolen's stunning book, *Color Me a Rhyme: Nature Poems for Young People* (2000), ready, the specific poems she wants to share already marked with sticky notes. She has assembled construction paper in various colors to use as cues for her students to brainstorm color synonyms. Her list of color words, chart paper, and working markers are at hand so that she doesn't waste a minute of instructional time when she models her own writing. This planning and organization lets Megan keep the minilesson to ten minutes; then her students are off to their desks to craft their own color poems.

Routines, predictable schedules, and organization make your day run smoothly. If you're a primary teacher and organization is not your forte, you may want to watch Linda Dorn's DVD *Organizing for Literacy* (2006), in which she and her colleagues address the practical issues of teaching such as scheduling, organizing center materials for students' independent use, and setting up classrooms with literacy corners intended to foster students' independence.

Discipline

No matter how much we plan in advance and no matter how well organized we are, there are bound to be children who test our patience and break our hearts. We lay awake at night, worrying about these kids. Some need extra support learning how to respect and get along with others. It's our job to help all children learn to be part of the learning community. When problems inevitably arise, the way that we handle those problems speaks volumes to our students about how much we care about them.

My first school memory is being one of forty first graders in a Catholic school in Birmingham, Alabama. We had to sit with both feet on the floor and our hands folded on our desk while Sister Mary Margaret marched up and down between the rows. I was a "good girl" and watched in horror as some of my classmates were sent to the corner or had their knuckles rapped with a ruler. (The only time I got in trouble was the day I wore too many petticoats!) Thank heavens corporal punishment is no longer part of classrooms today.

Contrast this with Kitty Strauss' response to a rowdy child who provoked his classmates with taunts while he tossed small erasers at them. She calmly took the child aside and talked to him. Listening closely, she figured out he was not feeling successful in his work and didn't want to be shown up in front of his peers. Kitty helped him with the activity but also coached him on ways to interact that would promote cooperation instead of competition. Listening and coaching are far more effective in changing behavior than harsh words or punishment and leave children with their dignity. Discipline will always be part of teaching, but we've come a long way in knowing how to address these challenges. The ways in which we provide guidance and discipline at school should be models for what we hope occurs at home.

We all have students who struggle academically and socially. Kitty had more than her share of them recently but was determined to face the challenge successfully. At the end of the year, she wrote, "My challenge has been to find ways to reach every student. We've clapped, rapped, and tapped more the past two years than at any time in my career. We had to start from scratch, and we still didn't quite reach the finish line I envisioned. But that's what makes teaching such an incredible profession: you get the chance to try to work a little magic."

If you're new to teaching, if you have a particularly challenging class this year, or if you just want some specific tips about how to "work a little magic," *Why Can't You Behave?* (2004), by Paula Rogovin is the most practical book I've found about positive discipline. Paula works intentionally to empower children to be in charge of their own behavior and learning. The book describes how to set guidelines for acceptable behavior, equitable discussions, and cooperation. She demonstrates how to hold students accountable and create logical and fair consequences. From the titles of her section headings—Pleasant Ways to Get Children to Do What They Are Told, Working When You're Tired, Dealing with Monday Mornings or the Day after Vacation—you know Paula is an experienced teacher with wonderfully sensible and wise suggestions.

I've observed many classrooms with all these elements—routines, schedules, organization, and positive discipline—in place. After working in these classrooms, substitutes often comment, "The class seems to run itself. I just needed to be there to steer it back on course when there was a small deviation.

Book List

Resources for Helping You Work Effectively Through Classroom Management

- [ ] *Qualities of Effective Teachers* by James Stronge (2007) (K–12)
- [ ] *Whole-Class Teaching* by Janet Angelillo (2008) (Grades 4–8)
- [ ] *Literacy Attendance* by Debbie Miller (2006) (DVD) (K–3)
- [ ] *Organizing for Literacy* by Linda Dorn (VHS or DVD) (2006) (K–3)
- [ ] *Why Can't You Behave?* by Paula Rogovin (2004) (K–3)
- [ ] *Class Meetings* by Donna Styles (2001) (K–8)
- [ ] *Classroom Management* by Irene Fountas and Gay Su Pinnell (VHS or DVD) (2005) (K–3)

Students knew their roles, their work, and especially how to treat one another." Have you ever watched a group of kids spend most of recess arguing about the rules of four square instead of playing the game? When the fundamental ground rules and structures are in place in your classroom, students can concentrate on learning. Your goal should be to create classrooms for learning and teaching that are physically beautiful and inviting but that also provide a structured and respectful community in which every student can blossom.

Ponder Box for Teachers

- Where would you place yourself on the Learning and Teaching row of the rubric that follows?

- What are your strengths and areas for growth in communicating with students?

- What are your strengths and areas for growth in discipline and classroom management?

- How do you help students learn the routines in your classroom?

Ponder Box for Coaches and Principals

- Where would you place your school on the Learning and Teaching row of the rubric that follows?

- Do you have clear expectations at your school about discipline? Do you have a written policy that teachers, students, and parents understand?

- What topics might you explore with individual teachers, grade-level teams, or the entire faculty?

- Which professional books or videos or DVDs might help you explore these topics?

Classroom Environment and Community of Learners (Teacher Rubric)

NOVICE	APPRENTICE	PRACTITIONER	LEADER
		Learning and Teaching	
☐ My classroom is teacher centered; my teacher talk predominates; the classroom is mostly silent or noisy with unproductive talk; I am usually at the front of the classroom or behind my desk; my classroom management is lacking or focused solely on discipline; students raise their hands and I call on them to respond; students primarily respond to short-answer questions	☐ My classroom is mostly teacher centered; my teacher talk predominates but I also lead some student discussions; the classroom is often quiet or sometimes noisy with unproductive talk; I sometimes meet with small groups; I am sometimes at the front of the classroom or behind my desk; my classroom management focuses mostly on discipline; I guide discussions and students raise their hands; questions and problems are usually directed to me	☐ My classroom is mostly student centered; the classroom is beginning to buzz with appropriate student conversations; I ask questions that facilitate learning; I use some intentional gradual-release techniques; I sometimes demonstrate, guide, or confer; my classroom management is mostly effective and focuses on student independence; I provide some opportunities for discussions, collaboration, open-ended questions, and problem solving; students are beginning to direct their conversation to peers as well as to me; students mostly respect and support one another	☐ My classroom is student centered; student talk is evident throughout the day in large- and small-group interactions, as well as during individual conferences; I intentionally use language and questions to facilitate learning; I teach responsively using gradual-release techniques; I usually demonstrate, guide, or confer; my classroom management is highly effective and focuses on student independence; I am a facilitator; I provide many opportunities for high-level discussions, open-ended questions, problem solving, partner and small-group work; students are respectful and supportive of others

Classroom Environment and Community of Learners (School Rubric)

Learning and Teaching

NOVICE	APPRENTICE	PRACTITIONER	LEADER
☐ The majority of the classrooms are teacher centered; in most classrooms, teacher talk predominates; classrooms are mostly silent or noisy with unproductive talk; teachers are usually at the front of the classroom or behind their desks; in some classrooms, classroom management is lacking or focused solely on discipline; in most classrooms students raise their hands and teachers call on them to respond; in most classrooms students respond to short-answer questions	☐ Learning is mostly teacher-centered in most classrooms; in most classrooms, teacher talk predominates but teachers also lead some student discussions; most classrooms are often quiet or are sometimes noisy with unproductive talk; in some classrooms, teachers sometimes meet with small groups; teachers are sometimes at the front of the classroom or behind their desks; classroom management mostly focuses on discipline; in most classrooms, teachers guide discussions and students raise their hands; in most classrooms, questions and problems are usually directed to teachers	☐ Most classrooms are student-centered; most classrooms are beginning to buzz with student conversations; in most classrooms, teachers ask questions to facilitate learning; in most classrooms, teachers use some intentional gradual-release techniques; in most classrooms teachers sometimes demonstrate, guide, or confer; in most classrooms, classroom management is mostly effective and focuses on student independence; in most classrooms, teachers provide some opportunities for discussions, collaboration, open-ended questions, and problem solving; in most classrooms, students are beginning to direct their conversation to peers as well as to the teacher; in most classrooms, students mostly respect and support one another	☐ Learning is student-centered in all classrooms; in all classrooms student talk is evident throughout the day in large- and small-group interactions, as well as during individual conferences; all teachers intentionally use language and questions to facilitate learning; in all classrooms, teachers teach responsively using gradual-release techniques; teachers in all classrooms usually demonstrate, guide, or confer; in all classrooms, classroom management is highly effective and focuses on student independence; in all classrooms, teachers are facilitators; teachers in all classrooms provide many opportunities for high-level discussions, open-ended questions, problem solving, and partner and small-group work; in all classrooms, students are respectful and supportive of others

Fostering Independence

In *The Daily 5*, Gail Boushey and Joan Moser (2006) remember how they used to teach several years ago: "We spent too much time managing [students'] behavior, planning activities, and putting out fires instead of teaching. We didn't have time to plan for excellent instruction that would meet our children's needs, nor did we have enough time for small groups or individual conferences" (5). As they read professional books and learned more, they began intentionally to teach toward independence by:

▶ Establishing routines and a gathering place for instruction

▶ Helping students choose just-right books

▶ Creating and displaying anchor charts about literacy behaviors

▶ Providing short, repeated practice intervals

▶ Using structures and signals for work periods and transitions

▶ Demonstrating correct and incorrect behavior

▶ Interacting and conferring with students

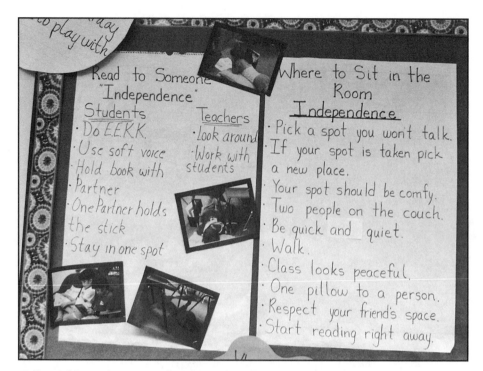

Melissa White and Karen Snyder Use Anchor Charts to Teach Toward Independence

Teachers like Melissa White and Karen Snyder use these ideas in the charts they create to promote independence during reading workshop. The charts are created with the students to anchor their understanding of independent behaviors. The teachers scaffold the practice of these behaviors by slowly building reading stamina with ongoing reflection and discussions with the students. Melissa and Karen also help their students create charts for other areas of literacy, such as independent writing.

There are three ways you can foster independence and move toward a student-centered classroom in which children can work independently by:

▸ Creating opportunities for choice

▸ Providing scaffolding

▸ Building stamina

Creating Opportunities for Choice

Are students in your classroom able to choose their writing topics and the books they read? Or do you rely primarily on whole-class studies of books you have chosen? Do you select the books and groups for literature circles, or do students get to choose? Do you provide starters for writing topics or do you present strategies that help students pick a topic and audience for their writing?

When students are given choices about what they read and write, they are more likely to want to practice and persevere as they encounter new challenges. Students become strong readers and writers when the scaffolding we provide is gradually removed as they become more independent. The more they practice reading and writing on their own, the more their skills and stamina grow and the more fluent they become. It's easier for students to stick with their literacy tasks if they care about their work. For both kids and adults, it's far easier to tackle a daunting writing project or read a hefty novel or dense nonfiction text when they've chosen the task and the topic interests them. The linchpin of caring is choice.

Brian Cambourne's *The Whole Story: Natural Learning and the Acquisition of Literacy in the Classroom* (1988), about the real-life learning of very young children, includes choice as one of the key conditions for learning. He acknowledges what others have theorized for a very long time—we all crave choice in what we learn and how we learn it. It's human nature. We want to learn about ideas and topics that pique our interest. Interest takes each of us on a separate inquiry in search of answers and energizes us to keep going. This same curiosity is inherent in young learners.

How can you accommodate this innate need for choice in your classroom? In reading instruction, you can provide a wide variety of books in many genres at appropriate levels. Within that wide range, you can guide your students to choose books that will engage them and keep them motivated to continue reading. Empower your writers by letting them choose their topics. Even if you are focusing on a particular genre, students can still choose the content and focus of their particular piece. For instance, when Megan Sloan launched a nonfiction unit, a trio of girls wrote about ballet; another group wrote about baseball; one group researched wolves; while other groups chose to learn as much as they could about the solar system, the rainforest, and deserts. They all became deeply involved in their research because they were reading and writing about topics they found fascinating.

My youngest son, Bruce, took piano lessons for many years. His interest started to wane once he entered middle school; friends, karate, and homework were demanding more of his time. His wise piano teacher, having picked up on Bruce's passion for Tolkien and the newly released *Lord of the Rings* movies, gave him the score from those movies to practice. Although the pieces were difficult, Bruce headed down to the basement to practice almost every day (without my nagging!). He practiced more (stamina) and his playing improved (new learning) because he was motivated.

Matching students' interests with the books they read and the topics they write about paves the way to engagement and independence in and outside school. An investment and passion for reading and writing doesn't come naturally to all children. Some need extra support and guidance in order to find books and topics that spark their interest. Your goal should be to have every child discover a book that is so engaging that her parents find her reading under the covers with a flashlight!

Providing Scaffolding

How do your students behave when you aren't in the classroom? Do they know the routines well enough to explain them to a guest teacher or visitor? Can they carry on while you chat with a parent in the hall? Do they depend on you for directions, or are they able to work independently for long blocks of time? We all want our students to be able to work independently, but this doesn't happen automatically.

In *Better Learning Through Structured Teaching* (2008), Douglas Fisher and Nancy Frey include a whole chapter about ways to build independence through gradual release—focused lessons, guided instruction, collaborative learning, and independent reading. You can also check in with students about their progress, ask questions, and provide support during conferences as they taxi down the runway before taking flight into independent reading and writing. Your goal is for students "fall in love with learning" so that they continue to read and write for the rest of their lives.

Here are some scaffolds you can use as you teach toward independence:

- Model your own passion and enjoyment.
- See that students read and write every day for sustained periods.
- Offer resources that will spark their curiosity and interest.
- Allow them to choose the books they read and the topics they write about.
- Provide explicit instruction that scaffolds students' learning and helps them become proficient readers and writers.
- Make your expectations clear.
- Monitor individual progress and provide targeted feedback.
- Help students set goals that will help them become independent.

Children learn to work independently when we give them responsibility. Donald Graves (2001) writes, "When you and your students take joint responsibility for the effective operation of the classroom, there is energy in the feeling of community that accompanies that accomplishment" (38). Students can take ownership of maintaining book areas and bulletin boards, cleaning up, helping one another, even writing thank-you letters and invitations. If you teach students how to sustain literature discussions and provide lots of modeling, even young children will stop looking to you for guidance and talk about books on their own.

To watch some master teachers support students' growth toward independence, buy or borrow the DVD *Developing Independent Learners* (2006), by Linda Dorn and Carla Soffos. These teachers reveal powerful layers of learning as they gradually remove their earlier scaffolding, moving from minilessons to literature circle discussion groups to reading conferences and eventually to peer conferences and independent practice. We too often ask students to be independent too soon. Linda and Carla help us see how we can support children's growing independence when we slow down, stay focused, offer tons of modeling, and then gradually withdraw our support.

The students in Ben Hart's classroom exemplify a refreshing sense of independence. When they enter the room in the early morning, they quickly put their backpacks and other materials away, read the morning message, take out their word sort materials, and begin their word-solving task. Ben doesn't have to remind them, other than in his written whiteboard message, what they need to do or why. Over the first few weeks of school, he provides streamlined explanations of routines and procedures that they practice and quickly internalize. Time is never wasted. During the daily reading and writing workshop, students work independently for twenty-five to thirty minutes, which builds their stamina and proficiency. Whenever they have a spare moment, students take out their independent reading or writing and continue where they left off. Their at-home reading and writing journals capture their learning outside school.

Building Stamina

When my daughter, Laura, was young, she was a gymnast. As a toddler, she went to a gymnastic class once a week. In first grade, the classes were twice a week, and we often found her upside down doing backbends and headstands at home. In middle school, she was on a gymnastics team, working for two hours a day, five days a week. That stretched to five-hour practices six days a week when she was in high school. Over and over and over, she practiced full turns on the beam, flip dismounts off the bars, and endless round-off back handsprings. The years of drills and practice led to harder and harder maneuvers, but only 10 percent of her success was the result of talent; the other 90 percent was made up of dedication, hard work, practice, and stamina. The same is true for any athlete, musician, dancer, or artist. And it's true for readers and writers as well.

Reading research shows a direct correlation between volume and achievement. In *What Really Matters for Struggling Readers* (2006), Richard Allington synthesizes a number of research studies about the importance of building students' stamina. Every teacher should be galvanized into action by his report that "the average higher-achieving student reads approximately three times as much each week as their lower-achieving classmates" (25). The implication is clear: in order to close the achievement gap, we need to get all our students, especially the lower-achieving ones, to read more each and every day, both at school and at home. Dick found that rate is critical to reading proficiency as well. "As a guide, 100 words per minute is an average silent reading rate for a second grader and 200 words per minutes is about average for a fifth grader" (36). Thus a proficient end-of-the-year second grader should be able to read and comprehend a book in the *Magic Tree House* series by Mary Pope Osborne and Sal Murdocca in about sixty minutes, and a fifth grader should be able read a novel like *Hatchet* (1987) by Gary Paulsen in about eight hours.

When I share this information with teachers, I often hear gasps and defensive remarks about how we want students to slow down and understand what they are reading. I agree wholeheartedly with the focus on comprehension. However, we need to think about all aspects of reading, and that definitely includes the volume and rate they need to reach in order to progress.

> # Ways readers can work on STAMINA
>
> ⭐ Make sure you are always adjusting the "movie in your mind".
>
> ⭐ Use your bookmark to mark a goal for the number of pages you will read during independent reading.
>
> ⭐ Read ahead a little bit to get excited about what's coming.
>
> ⭐ Talk with someone or write about your reading.

Sherri Ballew's Anchor Chart on Building Reading Stamina

Sherri Ballew knows this and presents several minilessons about building the stamina necessary to read (and write) for long stretches of time. She and her fourth graders also create an anchor chart they can refer to.

The research about reading holds true for writing. Lucy Calkins (1994) says, "One of our major goals at [the beginning of the school year] is to encourage children to say more, to sustain their work longer, to approach a text expecting it to be more detailed, and all of this means that we need to give children more time for writing than they know what to do with" (115). Early in the year, Megan Sloan's primary students get wiggly after only ten minutes of writing. But as Megan demonstrates tips using her own writing and they garner ideas from the fabulous books they read together, the students begin to take risks and write for fifteen or twenty minutes. Once they experience what it's like to have an audience gasp or giggle in response to their work, they head back to their writing with renewed enthusiasm. By October, her students are writing for forty-five minutes every day and groaning when the recess bell rings. Megan intentionally talks about building stamina all year long. If we want our students to have strong "literacy muscles" in order to support more challenging reading and writing tasks, we need to provide lots of exercise—lots of time spent reading and writing, beginning the first weeks of school. Donald Graves (2001) writes, "Long sweeps of time in a structured room allow for more independent, self-directed thinking, the kind of thinking needed today for the learners of tomorrow" (58).

When I visit Anne Klein's classroom, she and I can chat about her minilesson or a book we've read because her students are working independently. They are engaged in what they are doing, because they've chosen their book or topic and Anne's expectations are clear. Her student-centered classroom functions because she has scaffolded their independence by providing guidance and practice for each component of reading/writing workshop. For example, she models her expectations for peer conferences and provides

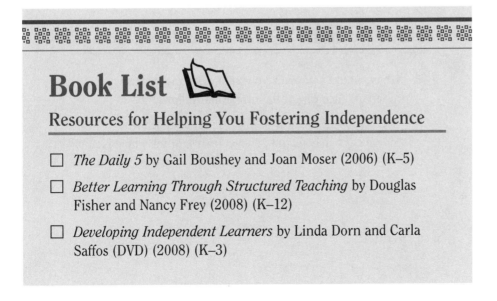

Book List

Resources for Helping You Fostering Independence

☐ *The Daily 5* by Gail Boushey and Joan Moser (2006) (K–5)

☐ *Better Learning Through Structured Teaching* by Douglas Fisher and Nancy Frey (2008) (K–12)

☐ *Developing Independent Learners* by Linda Dorn and Carla Saffos (DVD) (2008) (K–3)

many opportunities for guided practice before she expects them to confer effectively with their peers on their own. Knowing how busy many of her students are after school, she provides lots of time every day for authentic reading and writing to build up their stamina. Choice, scaffolding, and stamina develop the skills that lead to lifelong reading and writing.

Remember the book *If You Give a Mouse a Cookie* (1985) by Laura Numeroff? If you give students choices, they'll want to read and write. If they read and write a lot, they're going to build up stamina. If they have more stamina, they'll become better readers and writers. If they have more skills, they'll become more independent. And once they are more independent, they will become even more enthusiastic and eager readers and writers.

Ponder Box for Teachers

- Where would you place yourself on the Fostering Independence row of the rubric that follows?

- How can you help students build stamina as readers and writers?

- How can you help students work more independently?

- What kinds of scaffolding are you providing to help your students become independent readers and writers?

Ponder Box for Coaches and Principals

- Where would you place your school on the Fostering Independence row of the rubric that follows?

- Might you explore how to foster independence with individual teachers, grade-level teams, or the whole faculty?

Classroom Environment and Community of Learners (Teacher Rubric)

NOVICE	APPRENTICE	PRACTITIONER	LEADER
		Independence	
☐ I select topics for reading and writing; student work is mostly worksheets and workbooks; student engagement is minimal	☐ I occasionally offer students some choices of writing topics and some choices of books for independent reading; I assign many whole-class projects; students are sometimes actively involved in learning	☐ I offer some student choices for reading, writing, and inquiry; I am beginning to provide scaffolding based on students' needs; students are actively involved in learning; students work independently for short periods	☐ I provide many opportunities for choice to support engagement; I provide many opportunities for student self-selected reading, writing, and inquiry; I provide scaffolding based on students' needs; students' extended engagement leads to stamina and independence

Classroom Environment and Community of Learners (School Rubric)

NOVICE	APPRENTICE	PRACTITIONER	LEADER
		Independence	
☐ In most classrooms, teachers select topics for reading and writing; in most classrooms, student work is primarily worksheets and workbooks; in most classrooms, student engagement is minimal	☐ In most classrooms, teachers offer students some choices of writing topics and some choices of books for independent reading; in most classrooms, teachers assign many whole-class projects; in most classrooms, students are sometimes actively engaged in learning	☐ In most classrooms, teachers offer student choices for reading, writing, and inquiry; in most classrooms, teachers are beginning to provide scaffolding based on students' needs; in most classrooms, students are actively involved in learning; in most classrooms, students work independently for short periods	☐ Teachers in all classrooms provide many opportunities for choice to support engagement; there are many opportunities for student-selected reading, writing, and inquiry throughout the school; in all classrooms, teachers provide scaffolding based on students' needs; in all classrooms, extended engagement leads to stamina and independence

5

Becoming a Reflective Practioner

I feel honored to know, work with, and learn from so many outstanding teachers. Yet despite the professional excellence I encounter, I'm always struck by how shy and self-effacing most teachers are about the amazing work they do and the dedication they bring to their profession. The best teachers I know pour their heart, energy, and barely adequate salaries into honing their skills as professionals. They pay for classroom supplies, treats for their kids, stacks of children's books, and conference expenses with their own money. Stellar teachers open their doors to visitors, parents, and colleagues and share ideas freely. They read both children's books and professional books in order to improve their craft. I bump into them at workshops and see their cars in the parking lot long after their students have headed home. They're on committee after committee and are always the ones who bring in a box of doughnuts or a batch of brownies for their colleagues. These teachers enjoy being part of a professional community of learners and are more likely to replicate that experience for their students.

How many of these descriptors apply to you? If I asked you to raise your hand at a workshop, I know most of you would be too humble to let your expertise shine, but now, wherever you are as you read this, go ahead: silently admit that many of these qualities describe *you*! Outstanding teachers are part of a community of learners because of their ability to look inward and reflect on their practice and look outward for new ideas to implement and share with colleagues.

Looking Inward

Enjoy Life Outside School

It's important to find a balance between school and the rest of your life. If you've read *Teaching Essentials* (2008), I'm sure your heart lifted when, in the last chapter, Regie Routman urged you to have a life outside school. Amid the push for more accountability, the pressures of the plummeting economy, and the stress of ever-growing demands made by state and district boards of education, it's incredibly refreshing to read Regie's statement that staying later at school won't make us better teachers. She adds, "Spend most of your planning time thinking, not marking papers or creating elaborate centers" (129). Her message is to simplify, have more fun outside school, and keep your focus on your students while you are with them in school. When you hike with a friend over the weekend, take a dancing class with your significant other, or spend the weekend working in the yard, you come back to school reenergized. You can write about the waterfall, the new salsa dance you learned, or the smell of newly cut grass.

Remain a Lifelong Learner

When I asked Carrie who among the teachers she knows epitomizes a lifelong learner, she came up with a long list of names. One was Kitty Strauss. Carrie had heard about Kitty for years, but first visited her classroom about ten years ago as part of a language arts committee. Carrie was impressed with the way Kitty kept reminding the committee to remember the strengths and needs of *all* teachers, as she herself did with the students in her classroom. Kitty's practice has been exceptional for decades (no, she's not seventy years old!), but her expertise has not kept her from continuing her quest to learn and to improve her teaching. When Carrie met her, Kitty was learning about units of study within writing workshop. She read *Wondrous Words* (1999), by Katie Wood Ray, and went to hear Katie speak at a Colorado Council IRA conference (attending as many other sessions as she could as well). As Kitty modeled how to read like a writer, her students became better, more motivated, and more engaged writers. But Kitty still saw room for improvement, so she joined a book group that was studying the Lucy Calkins *Units of Study for Teaching Writing,* (2006). The next year, Kitty faced a number of social issues in her classroom, so she read *Choice Words* (2004), by Peter Johnston. She and a number of her colleagues made subtle changes in the language they used with students and began to see positive changes in their classroom communities. Last June, Kitty started a summer professional book club focused on building stronger, literate communities in the classroom. Kitty thrives on reading, sharing ideas, and learning. She's a powerful model for her students and colleagues.

Make Time for Reflection

School days are packed to the brim; any free time is immediately filled with preparation, meetings, or conversations and emails with parents. However, we also need to make time for personal reflection. Debbie Miller (2008) comments: "I learned the importance of slowing down and being present, of taking the time to think about and develop ideas, synthesize new learning, and write about what I had learned about my kids or myself as a teacher that day. And what it might mean for the days ahead" (20).

Carrie tells a story about her own journey as a reflective practitioner:

When I was first introduced to the writing workshop, while I was teaching first grade, my students and I were enthralled by the freedom and excitement student choice unleashed in their writing. I became a better observer of my students and learned a lot from them. But obviously I hadn't done enough thinking about my overall teaching. One day, in the middle of a social studies lesson, I asked the children to watch as I wrote their suggestions for the classroom store we were designing. Little Chloe piped up, "Mrs. Ekey, why do you always get to do the writing? You taught us how to write, but we only get to write during writing workshop." What a brilliant young thinker! She was doing more reflection than I was about writing across the curriculum! Soon after that, I began to weave writing into all content areas. I also began writing more myself. I started a teaching journal in which I reflected at least a few times a week on what I was noticing about student learning and recorded questions I was still pondering. That was my entry into reflective practice: I started to capture and reflect on the teaching decisions I was making. I moved from teaching "by the seat of my pants" to becoming more intentional and focused in my instruction.

Being reflective and responsive has also become part of my life as a literacy consultant and coach. When an administrator asks me to consult on literacy instruction at their school, I ask them to describe what their strengths and next steps might be. Many principals are puzzled. "Don't you just have a workshop you can bring us?" they ask. My response is, "Not really. I believe that it's important to design the workshop around your school's specific needs, much like I designed the instruction in my classroom around my students' specific needs." I'm asking those administrators to be reflective so that together we can design the best possible professional development that will meet their school's needs. Even in the middle of a workshop or demonstration lesson, I need to be reflective and responsive to teachers needs, revising my teaching along the way. Despite the demands on our time and pressure to achieve great things, administrators, teachers, and students all need to pause and become more reflective.

The staff development rubrics we've created are also a way for you to reflect on your teaching and set professional goals. After using the rubrics, Alicia Ngaropo wrote:

The teacher rubrics are a good starting place to help me focus and direct my teaching. Sometimes it's difficult to rate yourself as a teacher or even remember all the things that you actually do, but the indicators on the rubrics make the process easier. Highlighting the parts of the rubrics that I was already doing made setting my professional goals more focused. A colleague and I compared rubrics, discussed common areas in which we both wanted to do better, and made a plan to work on them together.

As I mentioned in the introduction, we do *not* intend these rubrics to be used as evaluation tools by principals; if they are seen as any kind of judgment, teachers won't use them honestly. Our hope is that in combination with the classroom stories and photographs we've provided, they will help you determine *what's working* and *what's next* as you strive to create beautiful and inviting classrooms in which you and your students learn together with rigor and joy.

Looking Outward

Some days, teaching can be joyful and exhilarating, filled with chuckles, hugs, and magical moments. Other days teaching can feel exhausting and frustrating, and we can become bogged down by negative energy, demanding parents, bureaucracy, and politics. Karen Ruzzo and Mary Anne Sacco (2004) compare a teacher's job with that of a television producer (and the TV producer comes out on top, by far): "Teachers not only produce but write, create, direct, and perform as host of a daily running show, all with only two commercial breaks" (8). Luckily, for most of us, the joy of our profession greatly outweighs the challenges.

As the century turned, Donald Graves became concerned about how overwhelmed teachers were feeling. Teachers everywhere were working so very hard and were so very, very tired. Traveling around the country, he interviewed teachers to find out what, out of all the things they did every day, energized and renewed them as teachers. He discovered that teachers had two main sources of energy: students (of course—they always energize us) and a sense of collegiality with other teachers. In *The Energy to Teach* (2001), Don emphasizes that each of us needs to assess all the things we are doing within our workday and then evaluate which ones are energizing and which ones are draining. From there, we can set a clear direction for what we want to remain constant and what we need to change.

Besides focusing on what gives us energy, there are five other ways we can remain energized as professionals:

- Read books about teaching.
- Write about teaching.
- Collaborate.
- Participate in professional development opportunities.
- Mentor others and become an instructional leader.

Read Books About Teaching

Since you're reading this book, you're probably already a reflective practitioner. Some of you no doubt lay awake at night thinking about your spelling program or worrying about a student. I'm fairly certain you see yourself as a learner and each year continue to add to your repertoire of skills. You keep up with recent children's literature and professional books, spending a fair amount of your own money doing so. I suspect you've already filled this book with highlighting or sticky notes. Many of you are members of adult book clubs or professional book study groups. You probably take note of your own strategies as readers and writers. Erian Leishman, an exemplary classroom teacher, loves to pull best practices from a range of professional books: "I love spreading my books all around when I start a unit. (I know I'm a geek but that makes me truly happy!)" The best teachers I know weave the new ideas they learn about into their classroom practices and reflect on the impact these ideas have on student learning.

In a three-part series called "Build Your Summer Reading List" (2006), by Brenda Power, on the Choice Literacy website, well-known writers of professional books reveal the one book they would recommend to colleagues for summer reading. This might be a great question to pose before your next staff meeting. Teachers could display their "book pick" in the staff room, library, or professional book corner with a card stating why they chose it.

I emailed several teachers and coaches I know with this question and received a fascinating variety of responses. Regie Routman's books were the most frequently mentioned: *Conversations* (2000), *Reading Essentials* (2003), *Writing Essentials* (2005), and *Teaching Essentials* (2008). Barry Hoonan mentioned *Readicide* (2009), by Kelly Gallagher, and Jodi Bonnette said that *The Comprehension Toolkit* (2005), by Stephanie Harvey and Anne Goudvis, was her pick since "it is practical, easy to use, and provides strategies for helping kids read informational texts, which is so important." Tanya Shahen said her favorite book was *To Understand* (2008) by Ellin Keene: "What does it mean to understand? This is the question floating around our school this year as we examine our practices as teachers through the lens of student learning. Ellin's new book brings current research to her already vast knowledge and expertise in literacy learning." The most intriguing response I received was from literacy coach Mimi Brown: "Because of the fiscal and political situation we're facing in our district, the book I need most has to get right to the heart of *why* we teach, instead of just *how*. *The Energy to Teach* (2001) by Donald Graves, would be the one book I would carry with me in my book bag right now, just so I can revive my own energy and share that passion for teaching with others."

JOIN PROFESSIONAL BOOK STUDY GROUPS

I've found that it's much easier to read a professional book with a colleague. If you're in an adult book club, you appreciate how much more you glean from a book when you discuss it with friends. Professional book studies can take place during lunch, before or after school, or even at a teacher's home (maybe with a cup of tea or a glass of wine). You might also watch exemplary teaching in action on some of the fabulous DVDs that have come out in the last few years.

Teachers at the Maplewood School, in Edmonds, Washington, have been conducting professional book studies for six years. The study group meets once a month for an hour and a half after school. Anne Klein, as the unofficial teacher leader, sends out reminders, prepares study materials, and distributes district clock-hour forms, and teachers take turns bringing snacks. They gather either in the staff room or in a classroom. (Anne usually brings a tablecloth and fresh flowers, which adds to the warm feel of the meetings.) They began with Regie Routman's *Reading Essentials* (2003) the first year,

Maplewood Cooperative School's Professional Book Study Group

followed by *Writing Essentials* (2005) the next year. After those two foundational texts, the group has gone on to study:

- *The Revision Toolbox* by Georgia Heard (2002)
- *Word Crafting* by Cindy Marten (2003)
- *How's It Going?* by Carl Anderson (2000)
- *Seeing Possibilities: An Inside View of Units of Study for Teaching Writing, Grades 3–5* by Lucy Calkins (DVD) (2007)
- *Strategies That Work* by Stephanie Harvey and Anne Goudvis (2007)
- *Lifetime Guarantees* by Shelley Harwayne (2000)

The books sparked great conversations that made the teachers feel part of a professional learning community and prompted them to implement new ideas. This professional sharing has opened up doors between classrooms, and teachers now visit one another's rooms and collaborate more often. One of the biggest outcomes is that teachers have now seen reading and writing workshop in action and realize they can do it! There's more conversation by teachers within and across grade levels about literacy and best practices. Teachers are also reading and sharing additional professional books on their own. Here are just a few:

- *Boy Writers* by Ralph Fletcher (2006)
- *On Solid Ground* by Sharon Taberski (2000)
- *Study Driven* by Katie Wood Ray (2006)

- *Inside Words* by Janet Allen (2007)
- *Craft Lessons* by Ralph Fletcher and JoAnn Portalupi (2007)
- *The 9 Rights of Every Writer* by Vicki Spandel (2005)

When she was principal of the Manhattan New School, Shelley Harwayne gave book talks on any new professional books that arrived at the school; teachers took turns reading the books and writing up one-page handouts of key points and quotes for their colleagues. What a great way to share ideas and keep current! Shelly says that one sign of a professionally alive community of learners is when professional articles begin appearing unbidden in teachers' mailboxes and they are heard talking about the children's books, adult novels, and professional books and articles they have read.

It's hard to keep up with everything we want to read (I often feel guilty about the unread professional journals that tumble over in piles in my office). That's in addition to keeping up with emails, Facebook, blogs, and other time-consuming ways to connect digitally. However, the one professional resource I read every single week is the online newsletter *Choice Literacy*. Brenda Power writes so well that I look forward to each introductory letter. Half of the articles and a few video clips are free; the rest require a nominal subscription fee. What I appreciate is that all the articles are only one or two pages and the video clips are no more than five minutes long and they are *practical*. You may want to share this online resource (choiceliteracy.com) with your colleagues.

JOIN ADULT BOOK CLUBS

Do you belong to an adult book club? I've always wanted to, but my travel schedule makes it difficult. Shelley Harwayne (1999) wrote about how the Manhattan New School initially offered one adult book club, which met once a month. As the school (and enthusiasm for the club) grew, there were soon three book clubs going at once. The groups meet first thing in the morning one day a month and are informal, voluntary, and joyful. I love that the tiles in the school's adult restroom list the title and author of every book their staff has read together!

Write About Teaching

The first chapter in Vicki Spandel's book *The 9 Rights of Writers* (2005) is called "The Right to Be Reflective." She describes how we are buffeted by noise, requests, information, and pressures, then gently reminds us not only to provide time for our students to write every day but also to find time to write and reflect about our teaching and our lives: "Commitment to reflection means having more respect for that internal monologue, whether we call it thinking, meditating, contemplating, or day-dreaming. It means abandoning our compulsion to feel dialed-up all the time. Giving ourselves opportunities to meander through the landscape of our own thought. For it is there in the quiet of our own minds, not on the evening news and not on the computer, that we learn to make sense of it all. It is there, in that internal world of the mind, that we develop the philosophy from which we write" (6).

WRITE REFLECTIONS

Do you have a writer's notebook? Have you thought about keeping a reflection journal or blog about teaching? Debbie Miller (2008) suggests that you jot down some thoughts for fifteen minutes at the end of the day (even just three times a week) and then reread your entries at the end of each month. It's amazing how much of what happens in a day or a week slips away and blurs. We can learn about our own teaching through our writing when it becomes part of our professional and personal lives and we begin to see ourselves as writers.

PARTICIPATE IN YOUR STATE WRITING PROJECTS

I spent one glorious summer in Seattle writing alongside other teachers at the Washington State Writing Project at the University of Washington. The first week, we were all convinced we couldn't write. By the second week, everyone was sure that *everyone else* in the group had talent. By week three, we eagerly awaited the next installment from our fellow writers and began to see that we, too, had stories to tell and began to see *ourselves* as writers. Kitty Strauss enrolled in the Colorado Writing Project twice and writes, "I grew immensely as a teacher of writing and as a writer myself through those two weeks of drafting, revising, conferring, and the reciprocal sharing of hearts and souls with other teachers. I finally published a poem in the Colorado language arts publication." Walking around in a writer's shoes is guaranteed to have an impact on how you teach writing to kids.

WRITE ARTICLES

Why not? You have expertise to share, and teachers love to hear about the "real world" of other classrooms. Plus, what a great way to model the writing process with your students! Last year, Cathy Hsu sent me her reflective teaching journal detailing how she implemented writing partnerships and peer conferences in her fifth-grade classroom. I was so impressed with her writing, the depth of her reflections, and how well she captured her evolving journey that I urged her to submit her writing to a professional journal. Cathy just emailed that her article was published in the October 2009 issue of *The Reading Teacher*! If you were to write an article, what would you want to write about? Who would be your audience?

WRITE A BOOK

That article could become a book. When I visited Ranu Bhattacharyya's kindergarten classroom, I was awed by the quantity and quality of the reading and writing her students were doing. I urged her to write about her teaching, and she's now joined the ranks of Heinemann authors. Her first professional book, *The Castle in the Classroom*, was published in 2010. I recently emailed Ranu and asked about the impact writing professionally has had. She said writing about her classroom has extended her community of learners; helped her bridge her long-term curricular objectives and daily teaching practice; and helped her see the continuous link between teaching with specific, targeted lessons and ongoing embedded assessment. Her instruction has become more streamlined, because she's become more conscious of time; writing has given her a clear idea of what was extra and what was essential. She's also become less resource dependent; her confidence in her own teaching has grown, and her primary resources and teaching tools are now the work generated by her students. A surprising side benefit has been the stature Ranu's writing persona has bestowed on her teaching persona—her students write more willingly than before, since they see she is asking them to do something that she does, too. Ranu has this advice:

> Several years ago, the energy within my classroom was so tangible that I wanted to open the doors and invite the world in! If you feel this energy and wish to write about it, start documenting your practice. Take pictures, save examples of student work, seek permission to use them. Discuss your ideas with your colleagues and mentors. Present at teacher workshops and see how your ideas are received. The more we share, the more global our community becomes.

Megan Sloan is another remarkable full-time classroom teacher—one who has managed to write three books in the last four years: *Into Writing* (2009), *Teaching Young Writers to Elaborate* (2008), *and Trait-Based Mini-Lessons for Teaching Writing in Grades 2–4* (2005). Megan says:

> Writing has changed me as a teacher in huge ways. It has made me a much more reflective teacher. I reflect on what to teach and why I am teaching it—I am constantly asking, "What value is there in the lessons I put before my students?" I also reflect so much more on ways to reach students. My writing forces me to think about things for extended periods of time. From this reflection comes trying new things, new ways, new strategies with students. Writing has caused me to look at student

work more critically, asking questions about what students write. What helped them elaborate? What practices in the classroom were most effective in helping students use interesting language? The answers to these questions help me plan my future lessons.

Writing about my teaching also changed me as a writer. I am much more specific. I am a much more "natural" writer because I am trying to capture lessons, experiences, and what I learn in one-to-one conferences. I sit back and think much more and am able to put my thinking down on paper with more confidence and ease. I am constantly watching the kids and reflecting while I write. I change what I write as I teach. My students teach me what I should be writing. Teaching, writing, and reflecting are all important parts of my life.

Writing helps you slow down and reflect on your teaching, and as you share your writing with others, your professional circle will widen and the response you receive will boost your energy and enthusiasm for teaching.

Collaborate

Teaching can be a lonely profession unless you find like-minded colleagues and feel part of a welcoming community of learners. Something electric happens when we can get together with a small group of colleagues to talk, read, write, and observe one another. That was certainly true for Carrie and her last teammate, who stretched Carrie to her outer limits of learning, immediately reenergizing her as a teacher. Carrie says, "I remember meeting her in the hall after school and beginning to chat about our learning experiences in our classrooms that day. One hour later, we were still in that hallway, sitting on the floor, deep into conversation about student learning." Collaboration can take place informally, as it did with Carrie and her colleague, or it can occur during grade-level meetings, demonstrations, team teaching, shop talk sessions, and vertical team meetings. Professional conversations are far more likely to happen if your school provides common planning time.

USE GRADE-LEVEL MEETINGS PRODUCTIVELY

It's hard to take time in the whirlwind of teaching to run to the bathroom (teachers have the highest incidence of bladder infection of any profession), much less make a quick phone call to a parent or talk to a colleague. When teachers attending one of my workshops have trouble settling down after lunch or after I've had them turn and talk, I understand perfectly. Teachers are starved for personal and professional connections.

Grade-level team meetings are one venue for collaboration. Are your team meetings filled with snippets of conversation about the upcoming back-to-school night, the resources you need for your next content-area units, reminders about health issues like the H1N1 virus, or what treats to bring for the thank-you breakfast for parent volunteers? Or do you and your colleagues bring student work from your current unit of study, analyze the students' strengths and next steps, then determine patterns of needs across your grade level, collaboratively planning instruction that will meet those needs? If you can answer yes to the last question, you're fortunate. When grade-level meetings focus on sharing teaching ideas and student work, you can tap into the expertise right down the hall and recharge your passion for teaching as part of a professional learning community.

At the Shekou International School, teachers intentionally use their grade-level meetings for professional conversations. Third-grade teacher Brian Morefield says:

> Effective meetings allow time to discuss/reflect on professional development that took place earlier. In our grade-level meetings, we share how we have incorporated the professional development in our classrooms and what worked or didn't work. This professional dialogue has been crucial in ensuring that our professional development doesn't end up as a packet sitting on our shelves but rather becomes learning that can be adopted incrementally and effectively.

Carrie recently observed the power of this type of collaboration in action. The teachers at a school she was working in wanted to help students improve their comprehension, so Carrie brought in a videotape of a guided reading lesson from one teacher's classroom (with the teacher's permission). This was the first time student work had been brought to a weekly team meeting. Immediately, the teachers became engaged, thoughtful, and reflective about what they noticed students *could* do and what next steps the students needed. They brainstormed possible instructional strategies—strategies they could use in their own classrooms. The forty minutes flew by. At the end of the session, the teacher whose children had been the topic of the conversation asked, "Couldn't we have this type of conversation at each of our team meetings or at least twice a month? We have learned so much from one another, and it will help all of us with our teaching. Besides, I really felt so much more engaged and energized today."

At another school, the kindergarten teachers had decided to use the Lucy Calkins *Units of Study for Primary Writing* (2003) in their classrooms but found them a bit challenging. The literacy coordinator, Stacey DuPont, knew how important it was for very young children to write, because doing so, in turn, supports their reading skills, so she promised the group she would investigate other professional resources that might be helpful as they launched writing workshop with their young students. She brought in *Talking, Drawing, Writing* (2007), by Martha Horn and Mary Ellen Giacobbe, and suggested they read and discuss the book. Because the topic was based on their need to learn, these teachers dug in. By the time Carrie arrived at the school, their children were motivated, engaged young writers and the teachers were anxious to tell Carrie about what they had learned.

At that same school, some astute primary teachers realized that the curriculum they were implementing didn't always align with the writing continuum they were using to evaluate student progress. Two of the teachers volunteered to create a document that would help all the primary teachers align these two valuable pieces of instruction, and the administration was happy to offer them the professional release time they needed. Again, the teachers determined an authentic need in the area of their own learning and figured out a way to collaborate in order to address that need.

ENCOURAGE CLASSROOM DEMONSTRATIONS AND TEAM TEACHING

Experienced teachers new to a school kept hearing about interactive read-alouds, turn and talk, and modeling think-alouds. They were curious about these strategies and asked the "push in" ESL/ELL support teacher if she would model some of these techniques in their classrooms. She readily agreed. The team teaching that resulted had not been formally set up by an

Team Teachers Karen Snyder and Melissa White Pour Over Student Writing Samples

administrator but took place because these teachers wanted to learn new strategies. One of them commented, "This is so much easier for me to understand and implement new ideas when you show me and then let me practice right alongside you." This is another example of how important it is for us to reflect on our practice in order to determine not just what we *do know* and *do well* but what we *don't know* and want to *do better.* By bringing our learning needs to the surface, we can read together and tap into the expertise of our colleagues in order to grow professionally.

When I taught in the federal Follow Through program, I felt very fortunate the years I had a full-time assistant. It's much easier to meet children's needs when two adults are in the room. I loved there being two sets of eyes watching and learning about and from our students. And when a student said something marvelous, it was great to be able to share the moment with another adult! At the American Embassy School in Delhi, Karen Snyder and Melissa White both taught second grade. Since they were already doing a lot of planning together and had similar beliefs, they decided to team-teach. They emailed me about their experience:

> One of the biggest aids to smooth team teaching is a common teaching philosophy. We knew our partnership would work because we both believe in a balanced literacy approach, have read similar professional books, and use best practices to steer our teaching. We spent many months planning and designing a classroom that would accommodate a double class of students with various learning styles and incorporate library nooks, student cubbies, alternative seating, a whole-group gathering space, teaching centers, and storage areas easily accessed both by our students and by us. Students get the best shot of instruction from our "tag team" instruction. One of us watches student behaviors and habits, while the other interacts with children during a minilesson. We both benefit from our individual strengths when we form small instruction groups to better meet students' needs. The children say they enjoy having two teachers in the room because they are able to get quick feedback and attention. In addition, they're able to form friendships from a larger pool of students. Teaching can be such an isolated job; team teaching allows us to benefit from each other's expertise and share the joys and diffuse the stresses of each day.

IMPLEMENT "SHOP TALK"

A few teachers in the PreK–2 division of the Hong Kong International School gather every Wednesday after school for forty-five minutes of "shop talk" in which they collaborate and share ideas related to math, grapho/fine motor

skills, and all areas of literacy. Leading and attending sessions are optional. Administrators provide a space and a cart of beverages and usually attend as well. Topics are posted in the faculty bulletin and teachers who have something to share sign up. Eliza Lewis and Danell Ricciardella hosted several sessions on word study and writing workshop that helped create the momentum for the school to create and adopt some common agreements on curriculum, instruction, materials, and assessments in literacy.

CREATE VERTICAL TEAMS

The intermediate teachers at the American Community School, in Abu Dhabi, are just beginning to implement the Lucy Calkins *Units of Study for Teaching Writing* (2006). Literacy coach Jen Munnerlyn organized "vertical" language arts committees for word study, reading, and writing. Each week Jen meets with a K–3 or 3–5 vertical team (grade 3 teachers cross over) that discusses, plans, and works on professional development together in one of those areas. Once a month, the entire K–5 vertical team comes together to discuss their work. Once each quarter, the whole staff meets to share what they have learned. Intentionally scheduling time for professional conversations ensures that teachers have time to talk and time to learn. Teachers also share ideas and questions with one another. Jen emailed me: "Just last week a fourth-grade teacher observed a fifth-grade teacher, a fifth-grade teacher observed me teach a lesson in a third-grade class, and a small group of teachers watched a video of a fifth-grade teacher and me conducting table conferences during the independent writing portion of another lesson. It's time consuming, but a great way to support sharing and learning. Last year we staggered language arts time in each grade so I can get to more classrooms each day."

The upper primary (third–fifth) teachers at the Hong Kong International School meet both within a grade level and across grade levels to discuss best practice, assessment and data collection, and curriculum scope and sequence and to share lesson-specific strategies. Colin Weaver writes,

> I find our meetings very helpful because I know where my students are coming from and where they are going in terms of literacy development. At the start of the year, I can immediately have deep, meaningful conversations with my students about their identity as readers and writers. Their self-awareness is only possible because all teachers are on the same page, focusing on process and strategies rather than just content.

Too often, teachers work in isolation. Teaching and learning are much more enjoyable in an environment of sharing and collaboration. Donald

Graves once said that you can tell the health of a school by the amount of laughter in the faculty lounge. In the schools I visit, that's certainly true. The schools that are the furthest along and the most joyful are the ones that have learned to balance the urgency of professional growth within a supportive and caring community. It helps to have a sense of humor!

CREATE LEARNING LABS AND MODEL CLASSROOMS

In *Learning Along the Way* (2003), Diane Sweeney describes how teacher observations have become increasingly more common and have evolved into three formats. *Peer learning labs* emphasize the host teacher as a learner rather than as an expert. Teachers use observation and reflection to work through challenges related to teaching and learning. *Student-centered labs* target specific aspects of student learning. Rather than focusing directly on instruction, the observing teachers collect student evidence and use it to unpack broader implications around teaching and learning. Both student-centered and peer learning labs are open, inclusive, and accessible and are developed and facilitated by a school-based coach who has been carefully trained to ensure that the process is rigorous and respectful. Learning labs play an important role in building a collegial school culture in which teachers think and learn together.

Model classrooms, in which teachers observe and reflect on effective instruction in order to implement that instruction with their own students, are the most common form of observation. Model classrooms provide an enormous amount of support in districts that are initiating a new instructional program or curriculum. They are also particularly useful in districts that have a large population of new teachers, because they provide a large degree of scaffolding and support. To learn more about learning labs and model classrooms, consult Diane Sweeney's newest book, *Student-Centered Coaching: A Guide for K–8 Coaches and Principals* (2010).

Once the intermediate teachers at the Hong Kong International School decided to adopt the Lucy Calkins *Units of Study for Teaching Writing, Grades 3–5* (2006), a consultant, Maggie Moon, developed lab sites at each grade level. The teachers are now able to see teaching and learning in action and to focus on one particular aspect, such as student conferences, in order to build their confidence and to develop some consistency across grade levels as they work toward common goals. They analyze student work, discuss what's working well, and share concerns. As a result, their writing program is stronger and there's a much greater sense of professionalism and collegiality.

ENCOURAGE PEER OBSERVATIONS

A favorite part of my job is getting to pop into classrooms and marvel at the amazing teaching and learning I see in action. I always wish the other teachers in the school were with me to take advantage of the experience and expertise right down the hall. In every school, time is a challenge; there's always a new initiative, new curriculum, or new ideas to implement. One way to stay sane is to take a step back, take a deep breath, and celebrate all that is *already* working—intentionally provide time for teachers to visit one another's classrooms. You can start gently, with after-school visits focusing on classroom arrangements, book corners, bulletin boards, and displays. As teachers begin to feel more comfortable being in other teachers' classrooms, they'll be ready to observe one another in action and focus on learning and teaching. (Strategies and protocols for classroom observations include cognitive coaching, developed by Art Costa and Bob Garmston, and "critical friends groups," developed by the Coalition of Essential Schools.)

The Singapore American School primary division (PreK–2) has just begun implementing formal (but voluntary) peer observations. Teachers tell the literacy coach about a strategy or lesson they'd like to observe, and the coach sets up a time with another classroom teacher. After the observation, the demonstrating teacher, the observing teacher, and the literacy coach hold a structured debriefing session. Literacy coach Louise Donaghey told me, "These informal sessions have been positive and productive and have sparked some long-term collaborative professional relationships. Peer observations are becoming more and more frequent as teachers try new ideas or hear about great lessons their colleagues have observed. This has made a

Kerri Shave Debriefs After Observing Lynda Scott's Kindergarten Classroom

huge impact on learning and transfer. It's so much more helpful to see a practice in action than to just read about it."

A school environment that promotes trust, mutual respect, and risk taking is conducive to peer observations. Everyone who visits the American Embassy School (AED) in Delhi, India, notices the sense of caring, camaraderie, and collegial support. Cheryl Perkins, who teaches first grade there, says, "In schools where teachers feel comfortable and valued and where doors are open, you find teachers going in and out of classrooms, saying, 'What a good idea! Can you show me how you did that?' AES is that kind of school."

In "Improving Relationships Within the Schoolhouse" (2006) Roland Barth outlines four aspects of healthy collegial relationships: educators talking with one another about practice; teachers sharing their craft; teachers observing one another's teaching; and teachers rooting for one another's success and offering help and support. He writes, "There is no more powerful way of learning and improving on the job than by observing others and having others observe us" (12). Visits have to be prearranged, confidential, focused (What am I going to look for?), and reciprocal and be followed by a conversation afterward. (If you're a principal, you could "practice what you preach" by having a principal from another school come observe one of your staff meetings and vice versa.)

The American School of Doha (ASD) has made a commitment to being a "learning-focused" school: "Learning is our core business and having a shared vision of learning is essential as we move forward towards providing the best possible 'learning experiences' for our students. Every decision we make and every plan that we implement has student learning as the essence of its intent" (in an email from a literacy coach at the school, 11/3/09). This is a huge paradigm shift; instead of focusing on teaching, teachers are now looking through the lens of learning. This shift influences decision making at all levels and encourages reflective practice for everyone. ASD and several other international schools are working with Fieldwork Educational Consultants on a protocol called "Looking for Learning." Administrators were trained first; last year teacher leaders and more recently (volunteer) classroom teachers were trained as well. Teachers invite colleagues into their classrooms to talk with students and determine what learning is going on in the moment. After each observation, observers share their observations about *student learning* with the teacher.

To keep this process comfortable, there's no evaluative aspect to the process. The protocol explicitly states, "These observations are not evaluative; the primary goal is to examine the *learning* that is going on within each classroom." As teachers and administrators spend time in classrooms talking to students, they ask, "What are you learning today?" "Why are you learning it?" and "What did you find difficult or challenging today?" These "looks at learning" are really just another form of peer coaching, using structured protocols for observing what learning is going on during any particular moment of the day.

VISIT OTHER SCHOOLS

Another way teachers can observe one another is by visiting classrooms in another school. It's important to get outside your comfort zone occasionally. Be sure to take paper and pen for notes, as well as your camera. If you're going to spend time in a single classroom, schedule the visit in the morning and bring lunch for the teacher as a thank-you. This gives both of you uninterrupted time to talk about the morning's activities. I always leave a thank-you note for both the classroom and the principal (or send the notes later), saying how much I appreciated the opportunity and mentioning some of the fabulous teaching and learning I observed. The first time I observed Sherri Ballew, during her first year as a teacher, I wrote up five pages of glowing comments and gave a copy to both her and her principal. I was blown away by how many aspects of literacy instruction, effective transitions, and minilessons she had in place the first month of school, as well as the level of engagement and learning that were evident in her classroom. I'm honored that she continues to let me visit and learn alongside her.

Visits between international schools are a problem because of the distance (not just a short drive, but a flight). However, a few years ago two international schools I work with did begin a learning journey together even though they are separated by hundreds of miles. The teachers in the PreK–2 division of the Hong Kong International School (HKIS) and the primary teachers at the International School of Bangkok (ISB) were both beginning to implement reading workshop. Both schools had curious, eager teachers who really wanted to learn more about this instructional approach. With support from administrators in both schools, a small group of teachers from ISB flew to Hong Kong to begin a collaborative learning effort.

The lower primary teachers at HKIS, based on the cohesiveness and rapport they felt with one another and their trust in Carrie's facilitation skills, took a huge leap of faith and opened up their classrooms to complete strangers. The first day, the ISB teachers visited classrooms and had small-group conversations with the HKIS primary teachers during their planning time. Carrie then facilitated a Saturday session on reading workshop. Later, the ISB teachers all agreed that being able to step into another teacher's classroom had impacted their learning. However, they found the chance to engage in a collaborative conversation with the classroom teacher about what he or she was doing and why to be even more powerful. Both schools, in collaboration, eventually hired Maggie Moon to establish lab sites at their schools.

Participate in Professional Development Opportunities

We certainly don't want to go to a doctor who hasn't kept up with new research and advancements in medicine. The same is true for teaching. Part of our job description is to be perpetual learners in our field. We are energized when we work in an environment in which we feel both challenged and supported and in which we can continue to learn. Schools can become centers for professional study by way of staff meetings, workshops and conferences, early release days, and retreats.

FOCUS STAFF MEETINGS FOCUSED ON PROFESSIONAL DEVELOPMENT

One of the missed opportunities for collegial conversations is the ubiquitous staff meeting. I remember too many unfocused faculty meeting that felt like a waste of time: they ran late and accomplished nothing. When workshops or faculty meetings are truly centered around students and learning, they can be invigorating and professionally stimulating. Just as children need to be part of a community of learners, teachers need the same sense of support and collaboration.

At the Singapore American School, teachers and administrators work hard to make staff meetings productive. They occur at a regular time (3:15–4:15 every Monday). The school's commitment to making this time sacred makes it clear that these meetings are important. Each month, two staff meetings focus on professional learning communities (PLCs), another deals with "housekeeping," and the final one is devoted to literacy. The agenda is posted well before each meeting and they stick to the one-hour time frame. Anything not addressed during the hour becomes a subsequent email dialogue. Jemma Hooykaas writes, "The predictable time, focus, and content makes the staff meetings enjoyable; I know why the meeting is being held, what will be accomplished, and that it won't run over the allotted hour. The respect the school shows toward teachers and our time makes the meetings wonderful, focused learning opportunities."

The staff at the Hong Kong International School chose their own professional development focus for a two-year period. They invited a consultant to their school several times over the two-year period to lead workshops, host lab sites, and build the capacity of the staff. During the workshops, teachers from all grade levels mingled to share ideas. Every other week, their faculty meetings provided time to reinforce best practice techniques that were established during the workshops. They also had weekly grade-level meetings to ensure continuity and success of the program across a particular grade. Each grade level had one or two representatives on the literacy committee, which made decisions about resources to use, units of study, assessment policies, and curriculum documents. Colin Weaver says:

> The benefits of this system were evident when we adopted the Lucy Calkins *Units of Study for Teaching Writing* (2006) several years ago. Some teachers piloted the units of study and gave feedback to committee members. Once we decided to adopt the units of study, we had a consultant come and run repeated lab sites at each grade level throughout the year. Lab sites were particularly useful because we were able to focus on one particular aspect of teaching writing (such as student conferences), in order to build teacher confidence and to ensure we were all using a similar approach. We are all now on the same page, striving for the same goal, and are able to share what is working well across grade levels, which further strengthens our literacy program.
>
> As a teacher, I loved having those professional conversations in both our formal and informal meetings. I felt I became a better teacher of reading and writing because I was able to bounce ideas off my colleagues and gain valuable professional development from literacy coaches and consultants. I benefited so much that I eventually became a literacy coach myself. Students also benefited as they began to hear common vocabulary used from year to year. They didn't have to relearn a new set of terms for the same concepts just because they were with a new teacher. I found my students' understanding of what good writers do began to flourish. They were able to articulate strategies during one-on-one conversations rather than retelling the story they happened to be working on that day. They also began to see clearly the connection between reading and writing. They now read from a writer's perspective and are on the lookout for new techniques to apply to their own narratives.

ATTEND WORKSHOPS AND CONFERENCES

I often ask teachers to tell me about a workshop they've attended that had an impact on their teaching and learning. Carrie Tenebrini remembered a visit I made to their school many years ago. She was on maternity leave but, not wanting to miss this important learning opportunity, joined her colleagues for the workshop. Carrie wrote:

> The best part of the presentation was when Bonnie gave her own "book talks" on both the professional reading and the personal reading she was doing. I remember thinking, *She's walking the walk, demonstrating for us*

*how we need to share ourselves with our students—share our passion for learn-
ing and reading, share our interests and personal lives. By bringing ourselves to
our teaching, we could have a greater impact on student learning.* I went home
that night and put together a list of all the professional books I wanted
to read. These books led me to other professional books, to the
Stenhouse website, to the Heinemann website, to the Teachers College
website, and the ideas I found there led me down many different roads,
to many conversations, collaborations, and learning experiences. All
from one professional development opportunity where the teacher led
by example.

My job as a consultant is to be practical—to provide ideas and strategies
teachers can use right away in their classrooms. I also want teachers to feel
affirmed for the strong teaching they're already doing, get excited by new
ideas, and continue to grow as professionals. I always booktalk the best new
professional and children's books. My goal is to leave a school buzzing with
excitement and new ideas.

Two years ago, when Jen Munnerlyn learned that she was going to be a
literacy coach at a new school in a new country, she quickly emailed me for
information about workshops or conferences on coaching. I told her about
Katherine Casey's summer workshop in Seattle. Jen writes,

I was the only international teacher in the course, but those three days
changed everything for me. From that workshop, I gained the confidence to jump into this new role. Probably more important, though,
Katherine showed me that asking for professional help from people you
trust (and possibly don't even know) is the key to continuing to
develop as a professional. My list of mentors is long and varied. Being
able to attend a workshop or conference hosted by one of these educators improves my work dramatically and reinforces my sense of being
part of a community dedicated to improving student learning through
excellent teaching practices.

Susan Hahn has this to say about the impact conferences have had on her
work as a teacher and literacy coach:

Even more than teaching in exotic locations and working with amazing
colleagues, conferences have propelled my practice to new levels. Like me,
many teachers reach some sort of plateau in their careers where teaching
is still rewarding but not inspiring. However, all it takes is one person and

one conference to ignite the fire and remind us why we embarked on this lifelong journey as teachers. Undoubtedly, many events have led me to the path I find myself on now, but it is the bends in the road that have made all the difference. Could it have been the first workshops on classroom-based assessment and developmental continuums Bonnie offered in Shanghai? The Bambi Betts workshop on differentiation? What about Carrie's workshops as she helped us understand the DRA and best practices in balanced literacy? Most certainly it was Carrie and Katherine Casey's two-year training program in literacy coaching, which showed all of us who enrolled the strength we have in ourselves and in each other—a network of like-minded educators. We attended a conference for international teachers and coaches for four summers in Seattle and encountered a myriad of mentors, including Ralph Fletcher, Debbie Miller, Stephanie Harvey, Katie Wood Ray, Regie Routman, Cindy Marten, Georgia Heard, Katherine Casey—the list goes on and on. The shared wisdom from these literacy experts reignited the passion in all of us. Sharing ideas with mentors and colleagues renews our passion and makes us all better teachers, coaches, colleagues, and friends.

IMPLEMENT EARLY RELEASE DAYS FOR PROFESSIONAL DEVELOPMENT

Researchers (and presenters) have long recognized the challenges of conducting staff development at the end of a long day of teaching. As a result, some schools have implemented early release days—weekly or monthly early dismissals or half-day releases several times a year—in which teachers have concentrated blocks of time for intentional professional development. In many districts, one weekly meeting is for whole-school professional development, one is set aside for grade-level meetings, another for work in vertical teams, and the fourth for individual or partner work in classrooms.

Administrators at the American School of Doha needed a way to support teachers who were beginning to implement the various school initiatives they had identified as crucial to improved student learning. The biggest barrier teachers faced in doing so was time; they often told administrators, "I know what we need to do, but there's not enough time." In order to provide the necessary time and establish an ethos of collaboration throughout their school, the school board approved a pilot two-year early release program focused on professional development—PACT (professional and collaborative time). Every Tuesday, all students left the campus at 12:30 (the instructional minutes lost were added to the end of the other four days each week). Consultants developed guidelines based on a common vision of and framework for collaboration. The literacy coach facilitated conversations to ensure vertical alignment.

The PACT guidelines emphasize the focus on improving student learning: "We will use PACT to collaborate within various, changing 'learning communities,' to grow professionally, and to collaborate together to enhance our planning, teaching, and assessment of student learning." The PACT goals are to:

- Improve student learning.

- Focus on student work.

- Enhance instructional practices.

- Increase professional conversations between faculty members.

- Effectively implement school improvement initiatives through collaboration.

These early dismissal days have had a definite impact on teachers and students at ASD. The change is obvious in the professional conversations that the literacy coach and principal overhear as they visit various teams.

Shekou International School provides a half day of release time every month, during which teachers work on schoolwide initiatives in curriculum groups and school improvement teams. This year the initiatives include differentiation, assessment, and curriculum planning based on the "understanding by design" framework from Grant Wiggins and Jay McTighe (2005). Teams have established norms and an identified purpose; the meetings are facilitated by teachers; and they focus on improving student learning. On a typical afternoon, teachers have professional conversations while they examine student work, critically assess rubrics' effectiveness, analyze curriculum documents for gaps, and share ideas from recent professional development experiences. There is a real sense of reflective achievement as goals are set, tackled, and eventually met.

Providing time for professional development sends an important message to both parents and teachers that the administration values learning. In both schools discussed here, professional development is focused, its laser beam pointed firmly on student learning. Most important, teachers have *time* to talk and grow through collaborative conversations. The ultimate benefit is that teachers are engaged in collegial professional development that leads to improved student learning.

INSTIGATE RETREATS AND GET-TOGETHERS

One of the best ways to bond as a staff is to get away from school together for a day or two. Becky Nelsen, the principal at Warder Elementary in Arvada, Colorado (Kitty Strauss's school), organizes a yearly two-day summer retreat during which teachers plan the upcoming year, examine test results, and figure out their focus and next steps. Even though the retreat is voluntary, at least 80 percent of the staff usually attends.

Diane Holt, the principal of Issaquah Valley Elementary, in Washington State, hosts informal discussions of great professional books at a nearby Starbucks, thus balancing high expectations with lower stress levels and supporting collegial friendships. (Sometimes Diane's parties are just for fun, like the cider-pressing party she hosted at her house last fall.)

When she was principal at Green Gables School, in Federal Way, Washington, Diane and her staff got away from the building for a one-day retreat before each school year began. Diane always devised a theme for the year that was a metaphor for the work they were doing together as a staff. For a great year when everything was going strong, she chose a flight metaphor, "Soaring on the Edges of Our Thinking." The staff just needed to stretch a bit, look a little further into the distance. Another year, when test scores took a dip, the theme encompassed three Rs—"Resiliency, Relevance, and Rejoicing." The staff worked to be resilient, focused on what was truly relevant, and rejoiced over what *was* working well. The year teachers began to conduct instructional coaching sessions, the theme was "To Sea with New Eyes." The staff went to Dumas Bay, looked out over the water, and envisioned how their work as coaches could help them revision teaching and learning. Diane writes: "I think themes help everyone hang their hat on whatever changes are going on that year. Each year I give a magnet to the staff that states the theme in big letters—many put it up by their work space and keep it as a reminder all year." Diane is a master at finding common ground, focusing on students and data, and using strategies like yearly themes to help bring teachers together as a community of learners.

Mentor Others and Become an Instructional Leader

During my very first year of teaching, Vivian Montoya taught next door; our classrooms had a connecting doorway. Each morning as we wrote our morning message on the board and organized materials and books for the day, we chatted about kids and teaching. In her quiet way, Viv mentored me. We were Follow-Through teachers (a federally funded program in effect then—sort of a Head Start for older kids) and had the luxury of working with a full-time staff developer, Helene Willis, who popped into my classroom one day each week to do some co-teaching, share helpful articles, answer questions, and marvel with me at the work my kids were doing. My goal in life was to be like Helene when I grew up. The program even flew me to Bank Street College for training my first year of teaching. I wish every first-year teacher (every teacher, period) could have that level of support and mentoring.

Some of you are fortunate enough to have a buddy in your building whom you can call on for ideas, commiserate with on rough days, and rejoice with on the days that shine. Others may have a wise and supportive literacy coach or principal who will squat down beside your students to marvel at their writing, roll up his sleeves and teach alongside you, and nudge you to excellence. I hope that all of you experience the gift of that type of support at some point in your career and that you, in turn, become that sort of inspiring mentor for others.

Louise Donaghey is the literacy coach for the primary division at the Singapore American School. Mentoring others has always been part of her journey. For example, when she met Pat Quick in 2005, Louise offered to mentor her as a student teacher. In her final year of college, Pat was assigned to Louise's classroom for a whole quarter. At that time, Louise was reorganizing her classroom library and implementing many of the literacy initiatives their school had undertaken. Pat learned alongside Louise, enthusiastic, passionate, full of questions and great ideas. Louise had to reflect on her own practices and look at her reasons for everything, from classroom management to the way she used resources and how she planned her units and minilessons. Pat is now in her third year as a first-grade teacher and is working on her master's degree. Several times a week she pops into Louise's office to ask questions about her current research project on writing strategies or tell a funny anecdote about one of her students. At other times, Louise is in Pat's classroom, team teaching, admiring student work, and discussing assessment results and evidence of student learning. Pat writes:

> It's hard to believe that it is already my third year of teaching first grade. I learned a lot about teaching through my student teaching and coursework for my bachelor's degree and now my master's degree. However, having Louise as my mentor has helped me apply the theories and best practices that I learned in my own classroom. Being able to discuss my ideas, concerns, or questions openly with a colleague has helped me become a more confident educator. Louise gives me insights from her own experiences and perspective. I enjoy being able to meet with her to discuss lesson plan ideas, curriculum, and assessment results. She is also willing to come into my classroom and team-teach literacy lessons. My students know her and are always excited to show her their work. Not only have I benefited from having Louise as my mentor, but my students have benefited from her expertise and our close, ongoing collaboration.

Louise Donaghey Mentoring Pat Quick

Carrie Tenebrini, the literacy coach at the Taipei American School, emailed me an articulate paragraph capturing the qualities of memorable mentors:

I think people who become successful mentor teachers or coaches have some important qualities in common. First and foremost, they have to be humble. They have to be ready and able to admit what they don't know and be willing to learn in the company of others. Because being a mentor or a coach means you are going to try to help people take their teaching craft to new territories, they first have to be willing to model how to venture gamely into the unknown; they have to demonstrate being a learner. Second, they have to be able to develop deeply respectful and trusting relationships with other teachers. Being a coach or a mentor teacher, ideally, means that you are not in an evaluative or supervisory role. The "power" the coach or mentor has is personal; their ability to effect change is only as good as their ability to make the teacher feel safe and comfortable. Building and maintaining trusting relationships requires constant care. It means being ready to meet each teacher where she is and help her get to the next step—the next rung in her personal ladder of professional development.

Cheryl Perkins exemplifies these qualities. She has a great sense of humor and she's the first to chuckle at herself. I tried to talk her into becoming a literacy coach because she's such a natural leader, but she was reluctant to leave the classroom; her love of children is evident in the way she talks about "her kids" and teaching. Even though she's remained in the classroom, Cheryl takes a quiet leadership role at school. She's a second mother to young teachers, taking teachers who are new to the school under her wing, answering questions about curriculum and students or even where to find cheap book tubs, a great restaurant, or the best place to buy rugs. Cheryl does informal teaching demonstrations when asked, volunteers for committees, and welcomes teachers into her classroom. She shares ideas as freely as the hugs she gives her students every day.

The first time I visited Cheryl, in Abu Dhabi, she had just invited all the moms of her students over to her house for coffee. The Emirate mothers were particularly touched, since many had never been invited to a teacher's house; they immediately reciprocated by inviting Cheryl into their homes. She was invited for dinners, birthday parties, and weddings and was "adopted" by one family who wept when she left. At her new school, in Delhi, she volunteers on the committee in charge of opening the school doors to the children from the poor but proud slum community across the street. Each Thursday after school, you'll find Cheryl at the hair-washing station, helping in the start-up library, or passing out school uniforms that the teachers provide for these kids. Her students from around the world keep in touch with Cheryl and invite her to their graduation parties and weddings. She reaches out to parents, to children, and to the community with open arms and an open heart. She epitomizes the best of teaching and affects everyone around her.

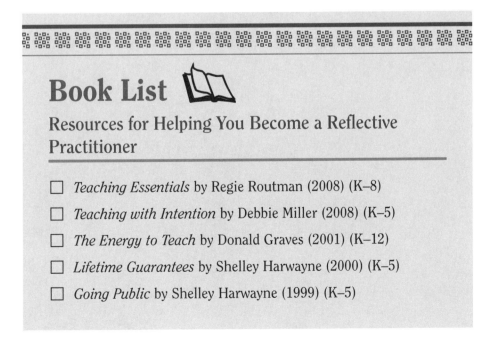

Book List

Resources for Helping You Become a Reflective Practitioner

- [ ] *Teaching Essentials* by Regie Routman (2008) (K–8)
- [ ] *Teaching with Intention* by Debbie Miller (2008) (K–5)
- [ ] *The Energy to Teach* by Donald Graves (2001) (K–12)
- [ ] *Lifetime Guarantees* by Shelley Harwayne (2000) (K–5)
- [ ] *Going Public* by Shelley Harwayne (1999) (K–5)

Carrie and I hope that you've picked up some new ideas from this book, that you have some new professional books on your "to read" list, and that you have occasionally caught glimpses of your own teaching reflected in our descriptions of exemplary classrooms. We hope you felt affirmed as you reflected upon *what works* in your classroom and set goals for *what's next*. We hope this book and the additional photographs and annotations on my website help you and your colleagues support one another as you continue to grow in your knowledge of how best to support your students and colleagues as members of a learning community

Ponder Box for Teachers

- Where would you place yourself on the Reflective Practitioner row of the rubric that follows?

- What are two ways in which you felt affirmed as you read this chapter?

- What are two ideas you could explore further or incorporate right away in your classroom?

- Is there a student teacher, a new teacher, or someone new to your grade level or school that you can mentor?

- What would be the focus of an article you might write or a presentation you might make at a conference?

Ponder Box for Coaches and Principals

- Where would you place your school on the Reflective Practitioner row of the rubric that follows?

- As you read this chapter, what are two ways in which you felt your school was affirmed?

- What are two ideas you could explore or incorporate right away as a school?

- How can you find more time to reflect on teaching?

- How can you help teachers share their ideas by writing or by presenting at conferences?

- How can you provide mentors for teachers new to teaching, new to a grade level, or new to the school?

- How can you open up the doors between classrooms? (Walkthroughs? Peer observations?)

- How can you provide more time for professional conversations in your school? (Common planning time? Early release days? Early dismissal?)

- How can you help see that grade-level and staff meetings focus more on professional learning and sharing?

- How can you support ongoing professional growth at your school? (Send teachers to conferences? Create a professional library? Support professional book studies?)

Classroom Environment and Community of Learners (Teacher Rubric)

NOVICE	APPRENTICE	PRACTITIONER	LEADER
		Reflective Practice	
☐ I work mostly in isolation and rarely collaborate with my colleagues; I participate reluctantly in required professional development activities and workshops	☐ I share ideas informally and collaborate with a few colleagues; I participate in required professional learning opportunities and book studies	☐ I share ideas and collaborate with my colleagues; I am part of a cohesive grade-level team; I exchange informal peer observations with a few trusted colleagues; I read material about best practices; I sometimes participate in optional professional development and book studies; I often share new ideas with peers and sometimes implement new ideas	☐ My school faculty is a collegial team; there is strong collaboration between grade levels; I exchange formal and informal peer observations with several colleagues; I actively participate in professional development and ongoing book studies; I collaborate, mentor other teachers, and take on leadership roles; I continually implement new ideas and seek to improve instruction; I am a reflective practitioner

Classroom Environment and Community of Learners (School Rubric)

NOVICE	APPRENTICE	PRACTITIONER	LEADER
		Independence	
☐ Teachers mostly work in isolation and rarely collaborate with their colleagues; most teachers participate reluctantly in required professional development activities and workshops	☐ Teachers share ideas informally and collaborate with a few colleagues; there is some cohesion with some colleagues or within some grade levels; some teachers participate in required professional learning opportunities and book studies	☐ Many teachers share ideas and collaborate with their colleagues; most grade-level teams are cohesive; there are some informal peer observations among a few trusted colleagues at some grade levels; most teachers read material about best practices; most teachers participate in optional professional learning opportunities and book studies; many teachers share new ideas with peers and begin to implement new ideas	☐ The school faculty is a collegial team; there is strong collaboration between grade levels; there are formal and informal peer observations within each grade level; all teachers actively participate in professional development and ongoing book studies; many teachers collaborate, mentor others, and take leadership roles; all teachers continually implement new ideas and seek to improve instruction; there is a school climate of investigation, exploration, and reflection

Appendix

Professional Books I Want To Read

As you read through this book and notice other books you might like to read, record them here. Code whether you want to read the book right away (R), later this year (L), or sometime in the future (F).

BOOK TITLE	AUTHOR	PUBLISHER/ COPYRIGHT DATE	INSTRUCTIONAL CATEGORY	NOTES	WHEN TO READ

Acknowledgments

Our biggest thanks go out to our patient families who put up with our overflowing piles of books, constant emailing, and perpetual guilt as we worked on this book. Special thanks to Carrie's husband, Glenn, who helped collect and organize our photographs, and Bonnie's husband, Steve, who patiently steps in whenever there is a technical crisis. And thank you to Bonnie's two sons, Keith and Bruce, who helped create her web-based database with their brilliant computer and artistic skills.

We would like to thank the following two colleagues who wrote an unbelievable number of thoughtful annotations for us that are posted on my website. This project could never have happened without the two of you reading and writing about so many professional books.

Laura Benson, Literacy Consultant, Denver, Colorado
Sandy Figueroa, Principal, Peña Blanca Elementary, Rio Rico, Arizona

Our project took many turns as it evolved into this book. We want to thank Lois Bridges, Leigh Peake, and Deb Eaton who supported us initially as we envisioned a series of books about literacy. Kate Montgomery patiently guided this book into its final evolution with vision and encouragement. Lynne Costa helped with the final layout and the difficult task of deciding which of the hundreds of photographs to include in this book. We're thrilled with the insert in this book that captures some of the beautiful classrooms far more effectively with color photographs. And we were awed by the editing skills of Alan Huisman. He managed to shrink our text to a reasonable length without losing our voices or meaning. We also want to thank Jennifer Yriondo (our local professional book rep) whose expertise about professional resources kept us up to date and eager to learn more. It's truly a joy to work with the Heinemann team.

We would also like to thank the following teachers, principals, coaches, and staff who patiently responded to our requests for classroom stories and examples, quotes, and photographs, which enriched this book immensely. We're constantly amazed by your dedication, commitment to your students and education, and openness to new ideas. You all are amazing teachers and reflective practitioners.

U.S. SCHOOLS AND TEACHERS

Anne Klein (and colleagues), Grade 4, Maplewood Cooperative School in
    Edmonds, WA

Megan Sloan, Cathcart Elementary, Grade 2/3, Snohomish, WA

Kate Morris, Horizon Elementary, Grade 4, Mukilteo, WA

Sherri Ballew, Sunnyside Elementary, Grade 4, Marysville, WA

Linda Lee, Willard Elementary, multi-age class (ages 6, 7, and 8), Spokane, WA

Mary Hammond, Willard Elementary, multi-age class (ages 6, 7, and 8),
    Spokane, WA

Doriane Marvel, Grade 1, was in Warsaw, now at Spicewood Elementary,
    Austin, Texas

Mimi Brown, Literacy Coach, Crestwood Elementary, Kent, WA

Diane Holt, Principal, Issaquah Valley Elementary, WA (formerly principal at
    Green Gables Elementary)

Sheila Medow, Kindergarten, Crow Island Elementary, Winnetka, IL

Vivian Montoya, Seattle, WA (was in Peru and Cairo)

Barry Hoonon, Grade 5 and 6, Odyssey School, Bainbridge Island, WA

Pam Pottle, Roosevelt School Grade 1 and Literacy Coach, Bellingham, WA

Helene Willis, Boulder, CO

Kitty Strauss, Grade 4, Warder Elementary, Arvada, CO

Becky Nelsen, Principal, Warder Elementary, Arvada, CO

AMERICAN COMMUNITY SCHOOL IN ABU DHABI (ACS), UNITED ARAB EMIRATES

Jen Munnerlyn, Literacy Coach

AMERICAN INTERNATIONAL SCHOOL OF BUDAPEST (ISB), BUDAPEST, HUNGARY

Carol Dulac, Grade 3 (now Grade 2 in New Hampshire)

AMERICAN SCHOOL IN LONDON, LONDON, GREAT BRITAIN

Julie Ryan, Principal

Suzanne Lituchy, Grade 3

Maria Puntereri, Grade 2

Jo Kember, Grade 1

Danielle Scully, Grade 2

Antonella Sassu, Grade 2 (now in Australia)

AMERICAN SCHOOL IN DOHA (ASD), QATAR

Tanya Shahen, Literacy Coach

AMERICAN EMBASSY SCHOOL (AES), DELHI, INDIA

Karen Snyder, Grade 2

Cheryl Perkins, Grade 1

Melissa White, Grade 2

Stacey DuPont (formerly literacy coach, now consulting in Saudi Arabia)

Ranu Bhattacharyya, Grade 4, (now at American International School of
    Japan in Tokyo)

ANGLO-AMERICAN SCHOOL, MOSCOW, RUSSIA

Susan Hahn, Literacy Coach (now at Saigon South International School in
    Ho Chi Minh City, Vietnam)

THE AMERICAN INTERNATIONAL SCHOOL OF MUSCAT (TAISM), MUSCAT, OMAN

Kerry Harder, Literacy Coach

Chad Johnson, Grade 5

Trish Tynan, Grade 2

HONG KONG INTERNATIONAL SCHOOL (HKIS), HONG KONG, CHINA

Ben Hart, Grade Assistant Principal, was Grade 3/4

Eliza Lewis, Grade 1, Literacy Coach

Colin Weaver, Grade 4

Danell Ricciardella, Grade 1 (now in Texas)

INTERNATIONAL SCHOOL OF BEIJING (ISB), BEIJING, CHINA

Fiona Sheridan, Literacy Coach

Mary O'Reilly, Grade 3

INTERNATIONAL SCHOOL OF BANGKOK (ISB), BANGKOK, THAILAND

Primary Teachers

SINGAPORE AMERICAN SCHOOL (SAS), SINGAPORE

Marian DeGroot, Upper Elementary Principal

Louise Donaghey, Primary School Literacy Coach

Jodi Bonnette, Intermediate Grade Literacy Coach

Kathy Cullen, Grade 4

Donna Hinton, Grade 4

Debbie Woodfield, Grade 1

Jemma Hooykaas, Grade 5

Pat Quick, Grade 1

Anita Gallagher, Grade 3

Karri Shave, Kindergarten

Lynda Scott, Kindergarten

SHANGHAI AMERICAN SCHOOL (SAS), SHANGHAI, CHINA

Erian Leishman, Grade 4

SHEKOU INTERNATIONAL SCHOOL (SIS), SHEKOU, CHINA

Treena Casey, Curriculum Director

Bob Dunseth, Director

Brian Morefield, Grade 3

TAIPEI AMERICAN SCHOOL (TAS), TAIPEI, TAIWAN

Carrie Tenebrini, Literacy Coach

Cathy Hsu, Grade 5

Kathy Sandler, Grade 4 (formerly at Shekou International School)

References

Akhavan, Nancy. 2006. *Help! My Kids Don't All Speak English*. Portsmouth, NH: Heinemann.

———. 2004. *How to Align Literacy Instruction, Assessment, and Standards and Achieve Results You NEVER Dreamed Possible*. Portsmouth, NH: Heinemann.

Allen, Janet. 2007. *Inside Words: Tools for Teaching Academic Vocabulary, Grades 4–12*. Portland, ME: Stenhouse.

Allington, Richard. 2006. *What Really Matters for Struggling Readers: Designing Research-Based Programs*. 2d ed. New York: Addison-Wesley Educational Publishers.

Anderson, Carl. 2000. *How's It Going? A Practical Guide to Conferring with Student Writers*. Portsmouth, NH: Heinemann.

Angelillo, Janet. 2008. *Whole-Class Teaching: Minilessons and More*. Portsmouth, NH: Heinemann.

———. 2005. *Making Revision Matter: Strategies for Guiding Students to Focus, Organize, and Strengthen Their Writing Independently*. New York, NY: Scholastic.

———. 2002. *A Fresh Approach to Teaching Punctuation*. New York, NY: Scholastic.

Barron, T. A. 2004. *High as a Hawk*. New York: Philomel.

Barth, Roland. 2006. "Improving Relationships Within the Schoolhouse." Alexandria, VA: Association for Supervision and Curriculum Development (March): 8–12

Bateman, Teresa. 2006. *The Bully Blockers Club*. New York: Albert Whitman.

Bauer, Marion Dane. 1987. *On My Honor*. New York: Clarion.

Bhattacharyya, Ranu. 2010. *The Castle in the Classroom: Story as a Springboard for Early Literacy*. Portsmouth, NH: Heinemann.

Boushey, Gail, and Joan Moser. 2006. *Simply Beautiful*. Holden, ME: Choice Literacy. (DVD).

———. 2006. *The Daily 5: Fostering Literacy Independence in the Elementary Grades*. Portland, ME: Stenhouse.

Brownlie, Faye, Catherine Feniak, and Leyton Schnellert. 2006. *Student Diversity: Classroom Strategies to Meet the Learning Needs of All Students*. 2d ed. Portland, ME: Stenhouse.

130

References

Calkins, Lucy. 2007. *Seeing Possibilities: An Inside View of Units of Study for Teaching Writing, Grades 3–5.* Portsmouth, NH: Heinemann. (DVD).

———. 2006. *Units of Study for Teaching Writing, Grades 3–5.* Portsmouth, NH: Heinemann.

———. 2003. *Units of Study for Primary Writing.* Portsmouth, NH: Heinemann.

———. 1994. *The Art of Teaching Writing.* 2d ed. Portsmouth, NH: Heinemann.

Cambourne, Brian. 1988. *The Whole Story: Natural Learning and the Acquisition of Literacy in the Classroom.* New York: Scholastic.

Cary, Stephen. 2007. *Working with English Language Learners.* 2d ed. Portsmouth, NH: Heinemann.

Casto, Karen, and Jennifer Audley. 2008. *In Our School: Building Community in Elementary Schools.* Turner Falls, MA: Northeast Foundation for Children.

Celic, Christina. 2009. *English Language Learners Day by Day K–6: A Complete Guide to Literacy, Content-Area, and Language Instruction.* Portsmouth, NH: Heinemann.

Chang, Maria. 2004. *Classroom Management in Photographs: Full-Color Photographs with Teacher Descriptions and Insights About What Really Works.* New York: Scholastic.

Chen, Linda, and Eugenia Mora-Flores. 2006. *Balanced Literacy for English Language Learners, K–2.* Portsmouth, NH: Heinemann.

Choi, Yangsook. 2003. *The Name Jar.* New York: Random House.

Clayton, Jacklyn Blake. 2003. *One Classroom, Many Worlds: Teaching and Learning in the Cross-Cultural Classroom.* Portsmouth, NH: Heinemann.

Clayton, Marlynn, and Mary Beth Forton. 2001. *Classroom Spaces That Work.* Greenfield, MA: Northeast Foundation for Children.

Cole, Ardith Davis. 2003. *Knee to Knee, Eye to Eye: Circling In On Comprehension.* Portsmouth, NH: Heinemann.

Coleman, Barbara. 2007. "Classroom Tours." Holden, ME: Choice Literacy.

Crawford, James, and Stephen Krashen. 2007. *English Learners in American Classrooms: 101 Questions * 101 Answers.* New York: Scholastic.

Cutler, Jane, and Greg Couch. 2004. *The Cello of Mr. O.* New York: Puffin.

Denton, Paula. 2007. *The Power of Our Words: Teacher Language That Helps Children Learn.* Turner Falls, MA: Northeast Foundation for Children.

Diffily, Deborah, and Charlotte Sassman. 2006. *Positive Teacher Talk for Better Classroom Management.* New York: Scholastic.

Diller, Debbie. 2008. *Spaces and Places: Designing Classrooms for Literacy.* Portland, ME: Stenhouse.

Dodge, Judith. 2006. *Differentiation in Action: A Complete Resource with Research-Supported Strategies to Help You Plan and Organize Differentiated Instruction-and Achieve Success with All Learners.* New York: Scholastic.

Dorn, Linda. (1999, 2006). *Organizing for Literacy.* Portland, ME: Stenhouse. (VHS or DVD).

Dorn, Linda, and Carla Soffos. (2003, 2006). *Developing Independent Learners: A Reading/Writing Workshop Approach.* Portland, ME: Stenhouse. (VHS or DVD).

Dragan, Pat Barrett. 2005. *A How-To Guide for Teaching English Language Learners in the Primary Classroom.* Portsmouth, NH: Heinemann.

DuFour, Richard, Rebecca DuFour, Robert Eaker, and Thomas Many. 2006. *Learning by Doing: A Handbook for Professional Learning Communities at Work.* Bloomington, IN: Solution Tree.

Echevarria, Jana, MaryEllen Vogt, and Deborah Short. 2009. *Making Content Comprehensible for English Learners: The SIOP Model.* 3d ed. Singapore: Dominie Press.

England, Crystal. 2008. *Divided We Fail: Issues of Equity in American Schools.* Portsmouth, NH: Heinemann.

Feigelson, Dan. 2008. *Practical Punctuation: Lessons on Rule Making and Rule Breaking in Elementary Writing.* Portsmouth, NH: Heinemann.

Fisher, Douglas, and Nancy Frey. 2008. *Better Learning Through Structured Teaching: A Framework for the Gradual Release of Responsibility.* Alexandria, VA: Association for Supervision and Curriculum Development.

Fletcher, Ralph. 2006. *Boy Writers: Reclaiming Their Voices.* Portland, ME: Stenhouse. (Audiobook).

———. 1996. *A Writer's Notebook: Unlocking the Writer Within You.* New York, NY: Avon.

Fletcher, Ralph, and JoAnn Portalupi. 2007. *Craft Lessons: Teaching Writing K–8.* 2d ed. Portland, ME: Stenhouse.

———. 2005. *Lessons for the Writer's Notebook, Grades 3–6.* Portsmouth, NH: Heinemann.

Fountas, Irene, and Gay Su Pinnell. 2005. *Classroom Management: Managing the Day and Planning for Effective Teaching.* Portsmouth, NH: Heinemann. (VHS or DVD).

Gaitan, Concha Delgado. 2006. *Building Culturally Responsive Classrooms: A Guide for K–6 Teachers.* Thousand Oaks, CA: Corwin Press.

Gallagher, Kelly. 2009. *Readicide: How Schools Are Killing Reading and What You Can Do About It.* Portland, ME: Stenhouse.

Gladwell, Michael. 2005. *Blink: The Power of Thinking Without Thinking.* New York: Little, Brown.

Graves, Donald. 2006. *A Sea of Faces: The Importance of Knowing Your Students.* Portsmouth, NH: Heinemann.

———. 2001. *The Energy to Teach.* Portsmouth, NH: Heinemann.

Harvey, Stephanie, and Anne Goudvis. 2007. *Strategies That Work: Teaching Comprehension to Enhance Understanding.* 2d ed. Portland, ME: Stenhouse.

———. 2005. *The Comprehension Toolkit: Language and Lessons for Active Literacy, 3–6.* Portsmouth, NH: Heinemann.

Harwayne, Shelley. 2001. *Writing Through Childhood: Rethinking Process and Product.* Portsmouth, NH: Heinemann.

———. 2000. *Lifetime Guarantees: Toward Ambitious Literacy Teaching.* Portsmouth, NH: Heinemann.

———. 1999. *Going Public: Priorities and Practice at The Manhattan New School.* Portsmouth, NH: Heinemann.

Hatkoff, Isabella, Craig Hatkoff, and Paula Kahumbu. 2006. *Owen and Mzee: The True Story of a Remarkable Friendship.* New York: Scholastic.

Heard, Georgia. 2002. *The Revision Toolbox: Teaching Techniques That Work.* Portsmouth, NH: Heinemann.

Hill, Bonnie Campbell. 2001. *Developmental Continuums: A Framework for Literacy Instruction and Assessment K–8.* Norwood, MA: Christopher-Gordon. (with CD-ROM).

Hill, Jane, and Kathleen Flynn. 2006. *Classroom Instruction That Works with English Langauge Learners.* Alexandria, VA: Association for Supervision and Curriculum Development.

Horn, Martha, and Mary Ellen Giacobbe. 2007. *Talking, Drawing, Writing: Lessons for Our Youngest Writers.* Portland, ME: Stenhouse.

Hsu, Cathy. 2009. "Writing Partnerships." Newark, DE: *The Reading Teacher.* March. 63, 2: 153–158.

Johnston, Peter H. 2004. *Choice Words: How Our Language Affects Children's Learning.* Portland, ME: Stenhouse. (Audiobook).

Keene, Ellin Oliver. 2008. *To Understand: New Horizons in Reading Comprehension.* Portsmouth, NH: Heinemann.

Kinesey-Warnock, Natalie 1992. *Canada Geese Quilt.* New York: Puffin.

Knowles, Trudy. 2006. *The Kids Behind the Label: An Inside Look at ADHD for Classroom Teachers.* Portsmouth, NH: Heinemann.

Kyuchukov, Hristo. 2004. *My Name Was Hussein.* Honesdale, PA: Boyds Mills Press.

Lane, Barry. 1993. *After The End: Teaching and Learning Creative Revision.* Portsmouth, NH: Heinemann.

Lester, Helen. 1999. *Hooway for Wodney Wat.* New York: Scholastic.

Lovell, Patty. 2001. *Stand Tall, Molly Lou Melon.* New York: Scholastic.

Ludwig, Trudy. 2005. *My Secret Bully.* New York: Tricycle Press.

Lundy, Kathleen Gould. 2008. *Teaching Fairly in an Unfair World.* Markham, Ontario: Pembroke.

Marten, Cindy. 2003. *Word Crafting: Teaching Spelling Grades K–6.* Portsmouth, NH: Heinemann.

McIntyre, Ellen, Ann Rosebery and Norma Gonzalez, eds. 2001. *Classroom Diversity: Connecting Curriculum to Students' Lives.* Portsmouth, NH: Heinemann.

McGrath, Constance. 2007. *The Inclusion-Classroom Problem Solver: Structures and Supports to Serve All Learners.* Portsmouth, NH: Heinemann.

Medina, Jane. 2004. *My Name Is Jorge: On Both Sides of the River.* Honesdale, PA: Boyds Mills Press.

Miller, Debbie. 2008. *Teaching with Intention: Defining Beliefs, Aligning Practice, Taking Action, K–5.* Portland, ME: Stenhouse.

———. 2006. *Literacy Attendance.* Portland, ME: Stenhouse. (DVD).

Minarik, Else Holmelund. 1978. *Little Bear.* New York: Harper Trophy.

Muth, Jon. 2002. *The Three Questions.* New York: Scholastic.

Nichols, Maria. 2006. *Comprehension Through Conversation: The Power of Purposeful Talk in the Reading Workshop.* Portsmouth, NH: Heinemann.

Numeroff, Laura. 1985. *If You Give a Mouse a Cookie.* New York: Scholastic.

O'Neill, Alexia. 2002. *The Recess Queen.* New York: Scholastic.

Osborne, Mary Pope, and Sal Murdocca. (various dates). *The Magic Tree House* series. New York: Random House.

Parker, Emelie, and Tess Pardini. 2006. *"The Words Came Down!" English Learners Read, Write, and Talk Across the Curriculum, K–2.* Portland, ME: Stenhouse.

Passel, Jeffrey S., and D'Vera Cohn. 2008. "U.S. Population Projections: 2005–2050." Washington, DC: Pew Research Center.

Paterson, Kathy. 2005. *Differentiated Learning: Language and Literacy Projects That Address Diverse Backgrounds and Cultures.* Portland, ME: Stenhouse.

Paulsen, Gary. 1987. *Hatchet.* New York: Simon and Schuster.

Pearson, P. David, and Margaret Gallagher. 1983. "The Instruction of Reading Comprehension." *Contemporary Educational Psychology* 8(3): 317–344.

Peterson, Ralph. 1992. *Life in a Crowded Place: Making a Learning Community.* Portsmouth, NH: Heinemann.

Polacco, Patricia. 2001. *Mr. Lincoln's Way.* New York: Philomel.

———. 2001. *Thank You, Mr. Falker.* New York: Philomel.

———. 1997. *Thunder Cake*. New York: Putnam.

Porcelli, Alison, and Cheryl Tyler. 2008. *A Quick Guide to Boosting English Acquisition, K–2*. Portsmouth, NH: Heinemann.

Power, Brenda Miller. *Choice Literacy*. (www.choiceliteracy.com).

———. 2006. "Build Your Summer Reading List." Holden, ME: Choice Literacy.

———. 2009. "A Place at the Table." Holden, ME: Choice Literacy.

Pransky, Ken. 2008. *Beneath the Surface: The Hidden Realities of Teaching Culturally and Linguistically Diverse Young Learners K–6*. Portsmouth, NH: Heinemann.

Ray, Katie Wood. 2006. *Study Driven: A Framework for Planning Units of Study in the Writing Workshop*. Portsmouth, NH: Heinemann.

———. 2001. *The Writing Workshop: Working through the Hard Parts (And They're All Hard Parts)*. Urbana, IL: National Council of Teachers of English.

———. 1999. *Wondrous Words: Writers and Writing in the Elementary Classroom*. Urbana, IL: National Council of Teachers of English.

Recorvits, Helen. 2003. *My Name Is Yoon*. New York: Frances Foster Books.

Rogovin, Paula. 2004. *Why Can't You Behave? The Teacher's Guide to Creative Classroom Management, K–3*. Portsmouth, NH: Heinemann.

Routman, Regie. 2008. *Teaching Essentials: Expecting the Most and Getting the Best from Every Learner, K–8*. Portsmouth, NH: Heinemann. (Website with video and DVD).

———. 2005. *Writing Essentials: Raising Expectations and Results While Simplifying Teaching*. Portsmouth, NH: Heinemann.

———. 2003. *Reading Essentials: The Specifics You Need to Teach Reading Well*. Portsmouth, NH: Heinemann.

———. 2000. *Conversations: Strategies for Teaching, Learning, and Evaluating*. Portsmouth, NH: Heinemann.

Ruzzo, Karen, and Mary Anne Sacco. 2004. *Significant Studies for Second Grade: Reading and Writing Investigations for Children*. Portsmouth, NH: Heinemann.

Schwarz, Patrick. 2006. *From Disability to Possibility: The Power of Inclusive Classrooms*. Portsmouth, NH: Heinemann.

Schwarz, Patrick, and Paula Kluth. 2007. *You're Welcome: 30 Innovative Strategies for the Inclusive Classroom*. Portsmouth, NH: Heinemann.

Scholes, Katharine. 1994. *Peace Begins with You*. Boston: Little, Brown.

Seuss, Dr. 1960. *One Fish, Two Fish, Red Fish, Blue Fish*. New York: Random House.

Sibberson, Franki, and Karen Szymusiak. 2003. *Still Learning to Read: Teaching Students in Grades 3–6*. Portland, ME: Stenhouse.

Sloan, Megan. 2009. *Into Writing: The Primary Teacher's Guide to Writing Workshop*. Portsmouth, NH: Heinemann.

———. 2008. *Teaching Young Writers to Elaborate: Mini-Lessons and Strategies That Help Students Find Topics and Learn to Tell More.* New York: Scholastic.

———. 2005. *Trait-Based Mini-Lessons for Teaching Writing in Grades 2–4.* New York: Scholastic.

Slobodkina, Esphyr. 1968. *Caps for Sale.* New York: HarperCollins.

Souto-Manning, Mariana. 2007. "Honoring Children's Names and, Therefore, Their Identities." *School Talk* 12 (3: 1–2).

Spandel, Vicki. 2005. *The 9 Rights of Every Writer: A Guide for Teachers.* Portsmouth, NH: Heinemann.

Stronge, James. 2007. *Qualities of Effective Teachers.* 2d ed. Alexandria, VA: Association for Supervision and Curriculum Development.

Styles, Donna. 2001. *Class Meetings: Building Leadership, Problem-Solving and Decision-Making Skills in the Respectful Classroom.* Portland, ME: Stenhouse.

Sweeney, Diane. 2010. *Student-Centered Coaching: A Guide for K–8 Coaches and Principals.* Portland, ME: Stenhouse.

———. 2003. *Learning Along the Way: Professional Development by and for Teachers.* Portland, ME: Stenhouse.

Szymusiak, Karen. 2006. "On Kidney Tables: Small Changes for Big Effects." Holden, ME: Choice Literacy.

Taberski, Sharon. 2000. *On Solid Ground: Strategies for Teaching Reading K–3.* Portsmouth, NH: Heinemann.

Tomlinson, Carol Ann, Kay Brimijoin, and Lane Narvaez. 2008. *The Differentiated School: Making Revolutionary Changes in Teaching and Learning.* Alexandria, VA: Association for Supervision and Curriculum Development.

Wiggins, Grant, and Jay McTighe. 2005. *Understanding by Design.* 2d ed. New York: Prentice Hall.

Yatvin, Joanne. 2004. *A Room with a Differentiated View: How to Serve ALL Children as Individual Learners.* Portsmouth, NH: Heinemann.

Yolen, Jane. 2000. *Color Me a Rhyme: Nature Poems for Young People.* Honesdale, PA: Boyds Mills.